MIRACLE MAN

One Family's Journey of Survival

By Kylie Paton

Miracle Man: One Family's Journey of Survival

© Kylie Paton 2021

All materials contained in this book are the copyrighted property of Kylie Paton. No portion of this book may be reproduced, stored in a retrieval system, or transmitted in any form or by any means – electronic, mechanical, photocopy, recording, scanning, or other – except for brief quotations in critical reviews or articles, without the prior written permission of the author.

Kylie Paton
PO Box 1125, Two Wells, South Australia 5501
Kyliepaton22@hotmail.com

Published and Distributed by Kylie Paton, Adelaide, Australia

Printed by:

 OpenBook Howden, 2-14 Paul St, St Marys, SA 5042
https://www.openbookhowden.com.au/

Cover Artwork by Chloe Joseph, Adelaide, Australia

Print ISBN: 978-0-6451029-0-1
eBook ISBN: 978-0-6451029-1-8

All quotes, photos and articles referenced in this book have been identified as quotes and their original source acknowledged.

To my husband, David.

*May the years ahead be smooth sailing,
and should another storm cross our bow,
may we stand strong in the knowledge that we are
united by faith and family for the long haul.*

Love always, Kylie xx

Contents

Foreword vii
Introduction ix
Chapter 1: Where It All Began 1
Chapter 2: The Waiting Game 7
Chapter 3: Mental Illness and the Legal Battle 11
Chapter 4: A Financial Lifeline 17
Chapter 5: New Beginnings or Déjà Vu? 21
Chapter 6: The Alfred 27
Chapter 7: The Trauma Ward and Angels 39
Chapter 8: Ghosts and Friendship 49
Chapter 9: Dead or Alive 59
Chapter 10: Rehab 71
Chapter 11: M31 National Highway 81
Chapter 12: Two Steps Forward, One Step Back 95
Chapter 13: Learning to Walk Again 113
Chapter 14: Country Air is the Best Medicine 125
Chapter 15: Creating a New 'Normal' 145
Epilogue 161
Acknowledgments 165
Mental Health Support Services 167

Foreword

by Peter Vanstan

Many people have written and spoken about the power of the mind.

The following story written by Kylie about her husband David highlights the strength of the mind when put under extreme stress. This story, spanning nearly ten years, reflects on not only the devastating physical and mental injuries that David encountered during two accidents on his bike, but also the financial and emotional trauma placed on the family during these times—which continues to this day. You will not only read about the extraordinary strength of David's mind and the battle for resuming a "normal" life, but also the strength of his family as they deal with day-to-day struggles in a world that's changed direction forever.

Although the mind is powerful, I believe that it needs a number of key components—focus, family, friends, and faith—to unlock its full potential. You will witness the ways in which these components affect David's survival and recovery.

David's focus and goal during recovery was always to get back on the bike. Some readers will find it bizarre that, although it was riding his bike that nearly took his life on two occasions, this was the driving force for his recovery. Biking was and remains his passion and continues to assist with his physical and, more importantly, mental health.

Although at times David may have felt alone along his journey, family and friends were beside him during every step. This story highlights the power of a strong and supportive network. David is blessed with the family and friends that have been by his side during not only the challenging and difficult times, but also during those moments of joy and celebration.

The theme of faith is weaved throughout the storyline. Kylie's strong faith (and that of her family and friends) was evident in David's recovery. The power of faith and prayer might not be measurable, but many would agree had significant positive impact on David's recovery.

The power of the mind is significant, and with these elements it can flourish. Fortunately, David has these rich ingredients that allowed him to overcome his near-death experiences. His story is a motivation to others as a reminder that no mountain is too high… even with a gradient greater than 20 percent on a road bike!!!

I would also like to acknowledge the wonderful care and treatment that David received from the staff at The Alfred Hospital, Melbourne and at Epworth Rehabilitation Centre, Camberwell. Your support in rebuilding David's body has allowed him to share his story and be a mentor to young students facing challenges of their own.

Introduction

MARCH 2016

My husband, David, was dubbed 'Miracle Man' by the media after his second encounter with death (yes, he's had more than one). It really is a miracle that he survived two near-fatal accidents within five and a half years of each other. But before I get into the details of our story, it might help if I introduce my family.

My husband of eighteen years, David (or Dave if you want to annoy his mum), was never your average guy to start off with—which is what probably attracted me to him at first and what frustrates me the most about him now. He grabs life with both hands and takes risks that most people would not. He has the gift of the gab and could sell ice to the Eskimos if he felt the need to. He has a wicked tongue that can shoot a person down in seconds, coupled with a fierce love and protectiveness of those he cares about. He would do anything for you, but break his trust and that's the end of the journey for you. He delights in baiting his mates on Facebook about football, a never-ending source of frustration for me. He loves to spend money, even when we do not have any, as his philosophy is, "we cannot take it with us when we die!" He is passionate about cycling and his kids. David would lay down his life for his children and has always worked hard to provide for his family.

As for me, I am the workhorse of the family. I hate being in debt and I love blessing others whenever I can. I have struggled with insecurity and self-doubt since I was a child and at times this has frustrated David to no end. I am loyal and trustworthy and would do anything for those I love. My children are the light of my life and I thank God for them every day. Even on the days when I want to lock them in their rooms and run away for a few hours.

We have been blessed with two amazing children, Kaitlyn and Joshua. As I begin to look back on our journey and write this story Kaitlyn is twelve and in her first year of high school, and Joshua is eight and in Grade 2. They are both excellent athletes and enjoy school, sport, and travelling around Australia on our family holidays.

David and I have worked very hard and achieved some great things in our time together. We built a business, lost everything, rebuilt our lives, and then lost it all over again, only to rebuild once more. We are incredibly blessed by our family and friends and this is something that we never take for granted. As a family we embrace our Christian faith and do our best to live good, honest, and faith-filled lives.

Life is good. For the first time in five years, since David's near-fatal cycling accident, we are gelling again as a family. It has been a long five years as we dealt not only with David's physical injuries but the much more difficult mental injuries. It is fairly common knowledge that Post-Traumatic Stress Disorder (PTSD) affects military and emergency service personnel, but most people don't realize that PTSD can affect anybody after a traumatic event. It can occur after an abusive relationship, a house fire, or, in David's case, an accident. It is one of those conditions that eats away at the person affected.

It changes who they are, how they act, and how they react. Couple PTSD with severe depression and panic attacks and you have a recipe fit to destroy a family. It nearly did ours!

Thank you for joining me on our journey; I hope it will inspire and encourage you.

—Kylie

CHAPTER 1

Where It All Began

In January 2011, we were in Adelaide for our annual sojourn to the Tour Down Under, which we have been attending since our wedding on 18th January 2003. Apart from missing a few years when the kids, Kaitlyn and Joshua, came along, we have been attending the Tour annually. That particular year we had convinced David's best mate and his family to join us, and our little group had grown to be a sizable force that descended on the Adelaide Caravan Park that hot January of 2011. The days leading up to David's first accident were filled with cycling, swimming, exploring Adelaide and its beautiful countryside, eating, and laughter.

It was Saturday the 22nd January 2011, and we were heading up to Wilunga for the day's cycling stage. It's interesting, looking back now, the details I can and cannot remember about that day. I cannot remember what we had fought about that morning, but I do remember being angry with David. It must have been a doozy, as I stayed angry with him all day. It was stinking hot, the kids were grumpy after a week of spending hours and hours in the summer sun watching the cycling, and I was not happy to be there.

I remember David going across the road to get some fish and chips for lunch whilst I was reapplying sunscreen on the kids. I had taken my rings off and put them in my lap before slathering the greasy sunscreen on their skin; but I forgot that I had done so until I stood up to put the sunscreen back in the bag and heard the metallic ping as the rings hit the ground and rolled away. I panicked when I could not find two of them—one of them my eternity ring, the most valuable ring I owned. I was devastated and just wanted to sit down and cry. Eventually we found both missing rings just as David was heading back with the fish and chips, and I breathed a sigh of relief.

The day dragged on and I just wanted to go back to the caravan park. When the stage was finally finished, we hiked back to the car where David and Jason (one of his mates over from Melbourne for the Tour) headed off on their bikes to ride back to Adelaide. I finished packing the car and the kids and I joined the queue of vehicles crawling their way back to the freeway entrance to head back into Adelaide. As we were waiting, I thought about how exhausting it was, holding onto my anger all day; I realized that David had gotten over the fight hours ago and that I needed to do the same. We passed David and Jason on the road, waving at them as we went past. I told the kids that we would go to the supermarket and then I would take them to the pool for a swim. We went to the supermarket and had just finished putting the food away at the caravan park when my mobile phone rang. I saw that it was David and answered, "Hey, Babe." The voice on the other end said, "Kylie, it's Jason. David is okay, but he's been hit by a car. You need to get down here now." I asked where they were, and Jason replied about 500 meters from the caravan park. I rushed the kids back into the car and hurried to the accident scene. Jason came over to the car to watch the kids while I ran over to David. To see him lying on the footpath in the fetal position, not moving, was an awful moment. A complete stranger wrapped her arms around me and said, "Everything will be okay." Unfortunately, everything was not going to be okay for a very, very long time.

We came to understand, pieced together by witnesses of the accident, that an elderly driver had run a red light, hit a learner driver in the middle lane, and then hit David, sending him head-first into a stone wall. The driver's family would also later tell us that he had had a medical episode, which is what caused the accident. The driver claims he never saw David.

The paramedics arrived and got David onto a stretcher and into the back of the ambulance. After the accident, a guy had blocked the left-hand lane with his tour bus; he picked up David's bike and asked where we were staying, and said that he would drop the bike back at the caravan park for me. There are still some nice people in the world and that man is one of them. I jumped back in the car to head the kilometer up the road to the Royal Adelaide Hospital where the ambulance was taking David. On the drive, I rang my sister in Melbourne in quite a state—which is unusual for me, as I am normally the controlled, 'can handle anything' person in the family. The kids and I arrived at the hospital in time to see David being taken out of the back of the ambulance. This was really hard for Kaitlyn as she idolizes her dad, and she was struggling to understand what was happening as an 8-year-old. Luckily, Joshua was too young to really know what was happening at that point in time since he was only 3 years old.

While the hospital staff was assessing David's injuries, I rang his best mate Pete to see if he or his wife Prue could come and pick up the kids so they didn't have to be at the hospital. Pete said that they were about an hour away but that Caz (Prue's sister) and her husband Shaun were closer and he would ring them and ask them to pick up the kids and the car and take them back to the caravan park for me.

When we were allowed into the cubicle where they were assessing David, he was conscious and was able to tell the kids that he was okay and not to worry. The fact that he had accepted the morphine they had given him told me otherwise. David does not do medication at all, so for him to accept pain relief spoke volumes. Not long after this, Caz arrived at the hospital and came in to grab the kids and the car keys from me. She said that Shaun was going to organize pizza for the kids, that Pete and Prue would be back at the park soon, and not to worry about the kids, just focus on David. She then told me to call her when I wanted her to pick me up.

Once the kids were safely on their way with Caz and Shaun, I busied myself with tasks that I could control, since I had no control over the situation in the hospital. I started making phone calls to our staff to organize drivers for the next week. You see, we were self-employed at the time of the accident and drove trucks delivering bread 363 nights of the year. We were due home in two days and it was obvious by this stage that we were not going to be able to go back to work yet, so I had to organize relief drivers. I had just finished sorting out drivers and notifying family of the accident when the doctor came into the cubicle with his report.

He told us that David had shattered his left elbow and would require surgery to put it back together. It's hard, looking back, to think that something that looked so seemingly benign would turn out to be so devastating.

Then he asked whether we had private health insurance. I looked at him a bit dumbly and finally asked why that mattered. He said that if we had private cover, the surgeon would come in the next day (Sunday) and perform the surgery. If we did not have private insurance, then it would be two or three days before David would get the operation.

To say I was shocked would be an understatement. My husband was lying in emergency battered, bruised, and broken and all the surgeon cared about was how much money he was going to be paid.

I told the doctor that we could not afford to be out of pocket but yes, we had private health cover. He said we would not be out of pocket and he would get David admitted and the surgery scheduled for the next day. By that time, it had gotten quite late and the nurses advised me that the kitchen was closed, so if David wanted any dinner I would need to go and get something for him. For anyone who is familiar with Adelaide, that is easier said than done at about 8pm on a Saturday night when you are not familiar with the city.

I rang Caz and asked her to come and get me, so I could get David some necessities and some dinner. She left Pete in charge of the kids, picked me up from the hospital, and we popped back to the caravan park so I could see my kids, hug them, tell them "I love you" and grab some gear to take back to David. Caz and I then started the hunt to find some takeaway food in Adelaide on a Saturday night. It took a while before we finally found a McDonald's. There was no parking anywhere near the restaurant, so I dropped Caz off, did a lap around the block while she ordered food, and came back to pick her up.

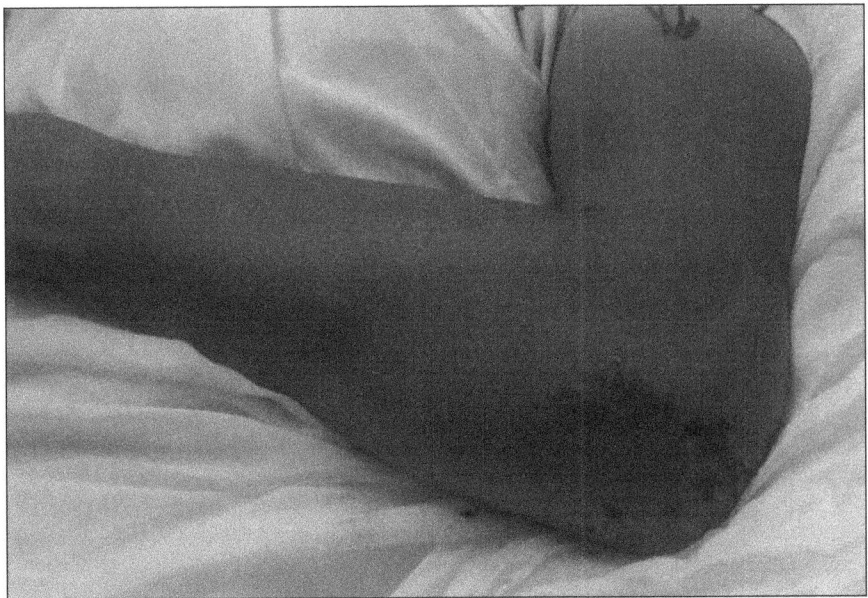

David's shattered elbow.

We finally made it back to the hospital emergency department to find David in a bad way. He had had an allergic reaction to the medication they had given him in my absence, and he was head down, feet up, and a deathly grey. It was an awful shock as he had been reclining reasonably comfortably and with good colour when I had left him an hour earlier. He obviously was not up to eating at that point, so Caz and I just sat with him for a while. Eventually they moved him to a private room, and Caz and I headed back to the park to try to get some sleep.

CHAPTER 2

The Waiting Game

Sunday morning dawned bright and sunny in true Adelaide form as I took the kids in to see Daddy before he went into surgery. They were very relieved to see him and gave him hugs and kisses before we left to go and watch the last stage of the Tour, trying to distract ourselves and kill some time. The nurse had told me that the surgery would take a couple of hours and they would call me when David was in recovery. We walked to the last stage of the cycling with our group of friends and watched the start of the race. After two hours of nervous waiting, I packed the kids up and headed back to the caravan park as I was too unsettled to sit at the race any longer. Three and a half hours later, I finally got the call to say he was out of surgery. They had had to put a metal rod and screws in to hold his elbow together and he was to be in a cast for the next seven weeks.

David slept on and off for the rest of that day, and during one of his moments of alertness, he sent the kids and I home to the park to try and enjoy what was left of our day. We tried to do so while he rested.

When we went in to see him on Monday morning, David was having problems with his left leg—he could not lift it or walk on it properly. I was very concerned, so I requested a full body scan. Since the accident, we had discovered that David had been catapulted into the stone wall head-first at 60 kilometers an hour—this fact was confirmed by his cycling computer, which registered him rolling down to the traffic lights at about 15kmh, then a sudden spike to 60kmh and the instant drop to 0kmh at the time of impact. The medical staff refused to do a scan, saying there was nothing wrong with him. They said, "He is fine, you can fly him home tomorrow."

But something was telling me not to put him on a plane. David agreed with me that he did not want to fly home; he wanted to drive home with the kids and me. I asked the hospital to do a scan once again on Monday afternoon and my request was denied for a second time. They discharged him from the hospital that afternoon and advised us we could drive home the next day.

Tuesday, 25th January 2011 was one of the longest days of my life. We left Adelaide early and had to stop every hour or so for David to get out of the car and stretch. David is a tall man, just shy of 6 feet 4 inches, and with his left arm in plaster and his left leg slowly swelling throughout the day, it was getting harder and harder for me to get him in and out of the car. We finally made it home after about 13 hours of travelling and I got everyone inside, showered, and into bed.

Wednesday was the Australia Day holiday and David was in a lot of pain. His left leg was quite swollen, and I was starting to get very concerned. I was not long out of bed when a knock sounded at the front door. I opened the door and there stood my guardian angels for the day. A couple of my girlfriends from church had rocked up and proceeded to unpack the car, wash the clothes, and clean the house for me whilst their husbands mowed and tidied up the yard. That day will always stay with me; they did in a few hours what would have taken me days to achieve. I was able to focus on getting David showered and fed whilst they dealt with everything else.

By Thursday morning, David was in extreme pain and I got him an appointment with our family doctor. The doctor took one look at David's leg and sent him for an ultrasound. The scan showed four blood clots in his calf that probably would have killed him had I put him on that airplane home! He was put on a blood thinner immediately and would remain on it for the next six months.

It still amazes me to this day that the medical staff completely ignored my requests for a scan on David. It was obvious that there was something seriously wrong and no one would listen to me. The consequences could have been tragic if I had listened to them and put David on that airplane home. I have never ignored my gut feelings since that day.

The months that followed our arrival back home tested our marriage, my patience, and our family. David was withdrawing into himself and struggling with getting through each day. He was unable to get himself to the bathroom without assistance, could not shower himself, dress himself, or feed himself unless the meal was able to be eaten with one hand. He was having panic attacks whenever he was in the car—one of a cyclist's biggest fears is being hit from behind, so the fact that he was hit from behind was playing havoc with his head. To make matters worse, he couldn't even remember the accident. He was having severe anxiety attacks, to the point that he could not get out of bed in the mornings. Our family doctor suggested we see a psychologist to give David some coping techniques as an alternative to anti-depressants. David had no interest in taking medication, which he felt was only going to mask the problem instead of helping him deal with the issues that were causing it.

CHAPTER 3

Mental Illness and the Legal Battle

I will never forget our first appointment with the psychologist. His first statement to us was that 95% of marriages do not survive a trauma of this magnitude. Not that it would be anybody's fault; he reminded me that David was not the same man I married anymore. Because he was at that time unable to give me the love and affection that I, as a woman and a wife, needed, the psychologist said that I would need to be very careful of the situations I put myself in. He said that all it would take was for another man to show me some affection and it would be very easy for me to stray. I thought, Gee, thanks for the vote of confidence! David and I would see the psychologist for the coming months, and he would assist David in finding ways to work through his panic attacks and bouts of anxiety, but life was still a very challenging journey.

David's moods would swing from remote but functioning to anger, frustration, and downright nastiness. I was trying to manage working three days a week, running our business, chauffeuring the kids to and from school and crèche, all while trying to keep our heads above water mentally and financially. We had just moved into our new home six weeks prior to the accident. We had no driveway, no landscaping, and many things still to be completed on the house. The builder was in the process of going out of business—something that we would not be aware of until weeks later when we were unable to contact him.

Considering the circumstances, I overruled David's desire for the kids to go to a Catholic primary school; instead, I considered the option of moving Kaitlyn from her Catholic school in Shepparton out to the local primary school a kilometer down the road. This would enable David to walk her to and from school instead of my 20-minute drive to and from Shepparton every day, which was starting to take a massive toll on me. Luckily both schools understood our circumstances and agreed that Kaitlyn could go for a morning to the local school and if she liked it, they would enable the transfer midterm, which was not usually permitted.

That Thursday morning, I took her up to the local primary school and left her with the Grade 1 teacher, who assured me if Kaitlyn got upset she would call me immediately. I headed back four hours later to pick her up as arranged, and Kaitlyn promptly burst into tears as soon as she saw me. My heart sank and I asked her what was wrong. She said, "I do not want to go home, Mummy. I want to stay here at school." The decision was made, and she would start at Toolamba Primary School the following Monday morning.

This was a small win in the big battle as funds were drying up, David was withdrawing further into himself, and my stress levels were through the roof. Something was going to have to give; I just was not sure what that thing was yet. Anyone who is self-employed understands the stress of dealing with insurance companies. Not only do you pay thousands of dollars a month to cover yourself in the event of something like this happening, when it does happen you will discover the lengths to which those insurance companies will go to avoid paying out on your policy.

I had contacted a local lawyer to seek some advice, as we had no idea what to do at that point in time. That lawyer referred us to a law firm in Adelaide that would be better able to help us, since the laws between Victoria and South Australia are so very different. That was the beginning of a journey through the legal system that would take three years to traverse and cause untold stress, tears, and heartache.

The other big decision I made in those days after the accident was to go back to church. We had never been a regular church-going family, but I felt the need to go that Easter Sunday in 2011. So, I dragged David and the kids to Generations Church in Tatura; I had been invited to a women's evening there the previous year which I had really enjoyed. I did not believe that weekly church attendance is required for a strong relationship with God, but I felt the fellowship and support that we would get from church would be invaluable. I was right. Whilst we did not get to church every week, I started attending a connect group with a group of older women who were my angels. They provided me with the love and support I desperately needed to navigate the hurdles I was facing every day. With my own parents farther away in Melbourne, having this support locally was life changing.

We would spend the next 12 months liaising with a lawyer in Adelaide to try and ensure that David was looked after and that we would recoup the massive financial losses that we were sustaining every day that he could not work. There were legal papers to read and sign, financial information to provide, hours of phone calls, and emails that never seemed to end. Within weeks of the accident, I knew that we were not going to be able to survive on David's Income Protection payments, the only insurance cover that the insurer was prepared to pay. Unfortunately for us, as we were self-employed, our income was split between the two of us; David's Income Protection would only pay us 75% of his half of our earnings—regardless of the fact that we had actually lost 100% of our income as it was all going towards paying relief staff. With this unexpected turn of events, I quickly realized that we were in deep trouble financially.

We had always looked after ourselves, accepting our victories and our failures, never expecting anyone else to bail us out of sticky situations. We had always just picked ourselves up, dusted ourselves off, and got on with what needed to be done to get back on our feet. We could not do that this time. Through no fault of our own, we needed help. David's parents had always told him that if we needed money we could just ask. It was one of the hardest things he has ever had to do. David gathered up his courage, rang his dad, and asked if we could borrow some money—which David assured him we would pay back with interest. His dad said yes immediately and arranged to deposit funds into our bank account that day. That lifeline would give us the breathing room to survive the next two years from hell and we were—and are—extremely grateful for that support.

As the months went on, David retreated further and further into himself. He lashed out at me verbally, to the point that on two occasions I told him he had to either go back to see the counselor, or pack his bags and leave. Thankfully, on both occasions he listened and sought help. You see, David had a history of pushing people away when he wanted something to end. Fortunately for him, I was not going anywhere, and I was not going to let him wallow in his own self-pity. The last thing he wanted to do was lose his family, but he did not know how to deal with the demons in his head and so he was reverting to old habits.

Looking back now, I am not sure how our marriage survived that stressful and trying period. I think, at the end of the day, it came down to the fact that I took my marriage vows very seriously and I was not going to let circumstances outside our control dictate our future. There were some very dark days during this time for our family. Days that I dragged myself through, leaning on the only thing I had left—God. No matter how dark the path was, He was always there beside me every step of the way. How do I know this? Because I am still here, my marriage is still intact, and I knew even then that we would come out on the other side eventually.

The next big challenge came in January of 2012. Our lawyer had advised that the insurance company required David to be assessed by all their specialists in Adelaide. He would need to be there for a week and see multiple specialists for testing, for five or more hours a day. We also needed to meet with our lawyer and go over the legal side of the claim for compensation that David was entitled to. So, we agreed to come over the week before the Tour Down Under to do what was required. Now, you should understand that for the previous 12 months, David had barely left the house. He would go up to the school to pick up and drop off Kaitlyn, into Shepparton for his specialist's appointments, and to the family doctor for his checkups—and that was pretty much it. He did not cope well with being away from home, and was battling severe depression and PTSD. I had no idea how any of us were going to cope with the challenge ahead of us.

So, in January of 2012 we went back to Adelaide, where our life had changed so drastically only 12 months earlier. I do not remember much from that trip, besides everyone being hot and tired from the long drive, and David being even more withdrawn than usual. What I do remember clearly is the absolute exhaustion on David's face each day when we picked him up from his numerous appointments; my breakdown in our lawyer's office when she advised us that our personal insurance company refused to pay out on either David's Trauma or Permanent Disability Policies, using the fine print to deny us any payment, and wondering how the hell I was going to be able to keep a roof over our heads; David's apprehension every time we drove past the accident site; and the distressing attitude of friends who did not understand David's withdrawn behavior. Overall, it was the longest three weeks of my life and I just could not wait to get home again.

The remainder of 2012 was a painful journey through the South Australian legal system as we learnt why so many marriages crumble, families are torn apart, and dreams are crushed. The games some insurance companies play to get out of compensating victims is appalling. The scrutiny is invasive and the delaying tactics to push families to the wall financially are atrocious. We were made to jump through hoops repeatedly—and we were the victims! The driver that hit David probably got a mild reprimand, had his car off the road for a few weeks whilst it was repaired, and then went on with his life as if nothing had happened whilst we were fighting for survival. We were at the breaking point financially. I could not afford new shoes for my daughter, let alone the presents we wanted to buy for her birthday and Christmas. I was stressing about how much longer I could hold off before I would need to put our home on the market. I was devastated. I was starting to fall apart.

CHAPTER 4

A Financial Lifeline

Just before Christmas of 2012 I realized that the only hope of saving our home was for me to try and get more work...as if I were not already stretched to the limit! I had been to Centrelink to enquire as to what payments (if any) we were entitled to, only to be told that we were eligible to claim Centrelink payments, but that any monies we were paid would have to be paid back once David received his settlement. I was stunned! We had both always worked and paid taxes, never asked for any assistance and the one time we were in dire need of help we would have to pay the money back! I walked out of the Centrelink office absolutely disgusted with our welfare system.

As I was updating my resume to apply for some work at the hospital, I recalled that my old boss (and longtime friend) Ange had changed roles. I messaged her and asked for her new title so I could update the information. What transpired next was one of those 'God instances,' as I like to call them—those moments in life when the strangest chain of events comes together to save your butt, and when you look back you are never sure how or why it happened, but you are very grateful that it did. Moments after sending the message, Ange rang me to ask what was happening. I explained the situation to her, and she gave me her new details. We continued chatting for a while when she paused and said, "You need to come back and work for me. I really need your skills as we are struggling to fill a Senior Process Specialist position." I laughed and said, "No way." I had no intention of going back to the corporate world and besides, I was not moving back to Melbourne—not even for a great job. She told me to send her my resume anyway, as she had staff in other states and did not see the issue with having someone based in Shepparton. I flicked it off to her later that day and did not think another thing about it.

I applied for numerous jobs in Shepparton and was unsuccessful in even getting to an interview for any of them. To say I was discouraged would be an understatement. I had never had trouble getting a job, from the time I turned 14 years old, work had always come easily to me. A couple of weeks later, I got a call from Ange to say her General Manager would like to set up a phone interview. I was shocked and asked how I could possibly take on a full-time role in the corporate world with everything happening at home. She told me that she had given her GM an overview of my current circumstances so that we were being completely transparent, and that he still wanted to interview me.

To cut a long story short, approximately ten weeks later I was once again a Telstra employee, working three days a week in Melbourne and two days a week in Shepparton on a six-month trial. If all went well, I would then commence full time in Shepparton with trips to Melbourne as required. Sunday nights were heartbreaking; my kids would stand in the garage, crying, as I left to head to Melbourne for work. I can't count the number of times I wanted to ring Ange and tell her that I just could not do it, but I knew that it was the best thing for our family—even if it did not feel that way at the time. Luckily that six-month trial turned into a four-month trial;

I was back home with my family, working for a great company, saved our family home, and could put shoes on my kids' feet once again. Since David still could not work, I had to resign myself to the fact that I would be the primary breadwinner for the foreseeable future.

It would take another 12 months before a settlement figure was put on the table by the insurance company. The figure was way below what our lawyer and barrister believed the claim was worth, and the next few weeks entailed negotiations for a more realistic figure. We were still struggling financially, and we were conscious that we owed David's parents a sizable amount of money that we desperately wanted to pay back. D-day finally arrived and our lawyer advised that the figure on the table was the last figure that they would offer and if we did not accept it, we would have to go to court. She advised that going to court would take at least another year, but more likely two or three years more, before settlement would be finalized. This had been dragging on for three years now. We were tired and over the whole thing. We just wanted to get on with our life. We were trying hard to create a new normal for our family and this was like a big black cloud hanging over our heads. We did what the insurance company was relying on and we accepted their offer. David and I both knew that our family would not survive if we kept fighting for the settlement he was entitled to. The money just was not worth it! So, we signed the reams of legal papers, paid back David's parents, and started to focus on figuring out what was next for us.

David's depression and PTSD were still a large cloud in our life, but we were working through it. He hid it fairly well most of the time and it was only when Kaitlyn told me there were mornings she had to wake him up and drag him out of bed to get her to school that I realized we still had a really big problem. We started camping again; between that and the counselling sessions that I insisted David and I attend, we started seeing an improvement. He did not want to take medication, but he was managing as long as we could get away every few weeks and if he could get out on the bike several times a week.

That in itself came with its own challenges as a rider's biggest fear is being hit from behind by a car. So, even though David needed to ride for his mental health, riding also caused anxiety and fear for a very long time. I don't know that the fear will ever go away, but he pushes through and does it anyway.

CHAPTER 5

New Beginnings or Déjà Vu?

Things continued in about the same way until 2015, which was a year of healing and new beginnings. We were finally starting to settle into our new normal and function as a family again. There were more good days than bad, and we were laughing again. Did we still have challenges to overcome? Yes; but then, do not most families? We just took each day and each challenge as it came and did our best with what we had to work with. We were blessed and I thanked God every day for that.

January 2016 would see us once again return to Adelaide for our annual trip to the Tour Down Under, albeit without the massive entourage of the last few years. We decided to stay in a new park that catered more to the kids and to really focus on making this trip about the whole family, and not just David and his riding. We had a great time and found the new park gave us the perfect balance we were looking for. We all came back refreshed and ready to see Kaitlyn commence her first year of high school and Joshua head into Grade 2.

My faith was stronger than ever. I had an amazing circle of women friends from church that had taken me under their wings and been my support and lifeline for the last four years. Although our church attendance was occasional, the friends we made there have been amazing. Their unconditional love for us and their support helped us survive a really tough period in our life. They continually reminded me that although we were "walking through the valley of the shadow of death"[1] we were not settling down for a nice long stay! Those words were so true. We were simply passing through and we did come out the other end eventually. Was it easy? No. Was it life changing? Yes! Did we learn some very tough lessons? Yes! Did we come out the other side wiser, stronger, and tougher? Yes. Would we want to do it again? No!! Life was finally good!

They say lightning does not strike the same place twice. They were wrong! If I thought the last four years had been tough, I was about to get the shock of my life.

Monday, 21st March 2016 started like most Monday mornings. David got up, gave me a kiss and told me he loved me, and headed off on his usual Monday morning ride with the boys in Shepparton. I went for a walk, came home and showered, and got ready for work. We had just started letting the kids have a little bit of independence; I would leave for the office whilst David was on his way home from riding, letting the kids stay home for about 10 to 15 minutes on their own. That particular morning I was running early and left about 20 minutes before David was due home.

I got to work and did not realise how late it had gotten until my phone rang. It was Kaitlyn telling me that Daddy had not gotten home yet, and she had to go and catch the bus for school and Joshua would be on his own. She said, "Daddy is not answering his phone." I told her to go to school, and that I would get our neighbor to look after Joshua and get him to school. By that point, I knew

---
1 Psalm 23:4

something serious had happened; David adores his kids and would never knowingly leave them stranded. I rang David's phones, and both went to voicemail.

I left the office, jumped in my car, headed to where David parked his car when riding with the boys, and felt my heart sink to my feet when I saw it still there. I knew then that he had been in a cycling accident again. What I did not know was where or when it had happened.

At that point, it was 7:35am and David should have been home at 7:10am. Shortly thereafter, the police called my phone and proceeded to confirm my gut instinct: David had been involved in a serious cycling accident. The police told me he was okay, but that they were airlifting him to Melbourne. I knew it was serious or else they would not be airlifting him. The policewoman said she believed that David had a couple of broken bones and some lung issues. How wrong she would turn out to be! She advised that she had the keys to a Jeep and what was left of his phone; I could either come to the scene and grab them or she would be back at the station in a couple of hours. I said I would come and get them, and she told me where the accident had happened.

As I was coming past the airport on my way to the accident scene, I saw the helicopter still there, so I sped into the car park and ran over to the helicopter where the paramedics who had transported him from the accident site were just finishing up. One of them helped me up into the helicopter, where I gave David a kiss, told him I loved him, and said I would meet him in Melbourne. He was unconscious and did not even know I was there, but I felt better for having seen him. The paramedic on the helicopter said they were taking him to Royal Melbourne Hospital and would be there in about an hour. I walked back to the car with the two paramedics who had transported David to the airfield. They joked with me about not letting David get another bike, at which I laughed and said that the one that got wrecked was his training bike, and his race bike was still hanging on the garage wall at home. One of the paramedics asked me if I was going home to drive over it so he couldn't ride that one; I said no, as then I would have to buy David a new one when he comes home from the hospital! Even then, I never lost my hope that David would come home and ride again.

Image of David's bike under the 4wd from the *Shepparton News*

Before heading on to meet them at the hospital, I continued to the accident site to pick up David's things from the police. As I arrived at the scene of the accident, I could see the driver of the 4wd in shock, waiting for his family to arrive. I spoke with the policewoman that had called me. She gave me the keys and the smashed phone and her details, telling me to call her if I needed anything. She told me that there had been a dead kangaroo in the middle of the road, but the boys hadn't seen it because the headlights from the car blinded them as they came over the rise. Eight of the ten cyclists went down; David was thrown onto the wrong side of the road and into the path of the oncoming 4wd. I would find out more details over the next few days as the boys came to see me at the hospital. To hear that David was trying to get out of the way of the 4wd when it hit him brought me to tears. I cannot even begin to imagine what was going through his head in those split seconds prior to the impact. The impact was so strong that the 4wd went over the top of David and his bike; he was left wedged behind the front wheels, still attached to the bike.

When the boys who were not severely injured realised what had happened, they immediately jumped into action. Luckily, one of the new boys to the group was a mechanic and he immediately grabbed the 4wd's jack and started jacking up the vehicle to ease some of the pressure off David, who was screaming, "Get this thing off me!" One of the other boys took his jersey off and wrapped it around David's head to try and stop the bleeding from his facial injuries, and sat there on the cold ground holding David's hand and telling him everything was going to be okay. They told me that David kept saying, "Kylie is going to kill me!" To which they replied, "Let's just worry about getting you out of there; Kylie will be fine."

The ambulance arrived, and David remembers hearing the paramedics say, "We cannot move him as he is still attached to the bike, we will have to wait for the rescue guys." It was 45 minutes before they were able to free David from his bike, get him out from under the vehicle, and on his way by ambulance to the airfield for the helicopter ride to Melbourne.

I left the scene of the accident and headed to my mum and dad's (who had recently moved to the area—what a blessing!); I thanked them for looking after the kids for the next day or two. As I headed out the door, my mum told me to make sure I packed a few things for David and myself. Mums are so wise; I had not even thought of going home to pack a bag. I was going to go straight to Melbourne.

I popped back to the office to grab my laptop and to ring David's parents and sister and let them know what was happening. I had to convince my mother-in-law to not go racing off to the hospital—she would not be able to see David anyway, and the last thing I needed was her getting in an accident as well. I also rang our daughter

Kaitlyn to let her know that yes, Daddy had been in an accident and was going to Melbourne, but he was fine. I told her that she and Joshua would be taken care of by their grandparents and I would call her later.

I headed for home to pack a couple of bags as the phones started going crazy with messages and phone calls. The news of the accident had been on the radio since 6:30am and friends and family were all ringing and messaging to make sure David was not involved. Responding to all of them would have to wait. With the kids taken care of, I headed to Melbourne to find David.

*[**Disclaimer**: Photos from this time are graphic and may be upsetting to some readers. Proceed through the next chapters with this in mind.]*

CHAPTER 6

The Alfred

The trip to Melbourne went by in a blur. David's best mate, Pete, had left an urgent message on David's phone after he saw a news article about the accident. I was able to get ahold of Pete and his wife Prue to let them know that yes, it was David that was in the accident and that I was on my way to the hospital. Pete said that they would meet me at the hospital. I told him not to be silly—he was at work—but he would not listen to me. Pete also offered to post something on Facebook to alleviate some of the pressure, to which I agreed. News of the accident was already all over the news, TV, radio, and social media. Pete posted the link to the accident article and let our friends know it was David in the accident and we would update them all as soon as we knew more.

Peter's post at 10:37am said:
   Hi everyone, our thoughts for David Paton, Kylie Paton and family…It is David that has been airlifted to hospital in

Melbourne! We will use this link for updates. Kylie does not know much at moment…So will keep you posted!

David's dad rang and told me that David had been taken to the Alfred Hospital and that they had spelled his last name wrong—Taton instead of Paton. Ironically, this would turn out to be a blessing as it bought me some time before the media frenzy started. It was at this point that I pulled off the highway and posted an update on Pete's Facebook post as I could not keep up with all the phone calls.

My post at 10:50am said:
Hey guys, thank you for all your prayers and support.
I would not normally do this over Facebook, but I know everyone is worried about David and this is the quickest way to update you all. He is in intensive care in an induced coma, with multiple injuries and fractures. I am on my way to the hospital now and will update you all later once I know more. I really appreciate everyone's support. Thank you.
Love, Kylie

I spent the rest of the trip to Melbourne on the phone with my boss and managers, who all said the same thing: "Forget about work, let us know what you need, and we will organize it for you. You have our complete support and do not hesitate to call if you need anything at all." This made a huge difference; knowing that was one less thing I had to worry about.

I finally arrived at the hospital around 1pm. Pete and Prue had arrived at the emergency department about ten minutes earlier and Pete had already sorted out all the paperwork for me, including fixing the spelling of our surname. One of the great things about having a mate that has been in your life since the age of 12 is that they know everything about you, things even your own mother does not know.

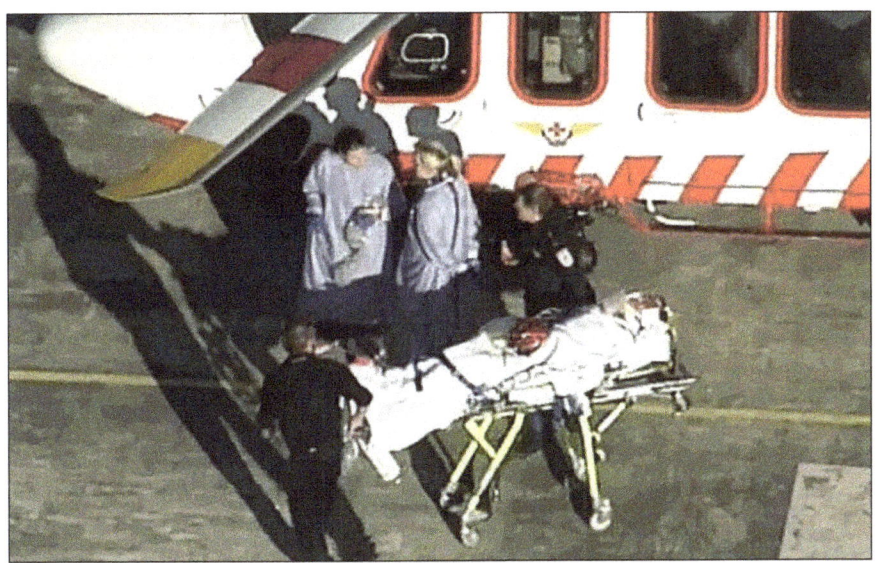

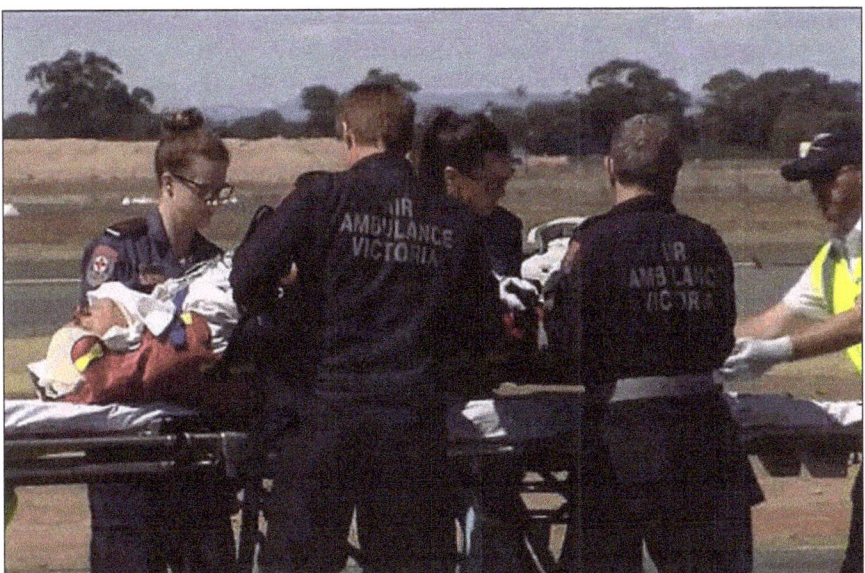

Photos courtesy of *9 News*

We were taken into a private waiting room and told the doctors would be in shortly. I am not sure how long we sat there. When the emergency doctors arrived, they introduced themselves to me and then the first thing they said was that they were really worried about the brain injury and the spinal fractures—if the spinal cord was impacted, those were the two things that they would not be able to fix. I knew that if David was going to have serious brain damage or be paralyzed, he would not want to live like that. It was at that point I began to pray. "Lord, if that's the case, please take David home now. If your will is that he survives, please give us a miracle and help these doctors save my husband's life."

The doctors told me that David was briefly conscious enough to answer a couple of questions before slipping unconscious again. They said he was in an induced coma to keep him immobilized and that both his lungs had collapsed. David had machines breathing for him and he had internal bleeding, which they were trying to stop without having to operate just yet. They really wanted to stabilize him before taking him into surgery, if possible. David had broken many bones, including his wrist, leg, ribs, and pelvis (and that list would grow as they got more scan results back). He was receiving blood transfusions to try and replace the significant blood loss he had sustained and as soon as they stabilized him, they would transfer him up to the Intensive Care Unit (ICU).

Once the doctors left, I shed my first tears that day. Pete rang Mum and Dad Paton and gave them the update. He told them there was no point coming in at the moment, as no-one could see David, and told them we would call them again as soon as we knew more. Just then the nurse came and told us that we could come in and see David briefly. We went into the emergency area where they were working on David. They had him covered so that we could not see all the damage. I gave him a kiss on the forehead, told him I loved him, and let Pete and Prue see him for a moment. The nurse told us to go and get something to eat; they would be moving him to ICU shortly and we could meet him up there.

We went to the cafeteria and grabbed something to eat—not that any of us felt like eating, but we knew it was going to be a while before there was any news (good or bad). We went and sat outside; it was a beautiful day and we all needed the fresh air and sunshine after the smells and sounds of the emergency department. Whilst we were eating, my boss Ange rang me again to see how I was holding up. She told me that one of the directors in Queensland had rung one of the general managers in Melbourne to organize some accommodation near the hospital for the next two nights. My boss asked if that would be helpful. I burst into tears and said, "Yes, that would be amazing." I had not even thought about what I was going to do about accommodation, much less any other details beyond the present moment. Ange told me to leave it to her; she would organize the accommodation and send me the details, and just put it all on my company card. I was completely overwhelmed by the generosity and thoughtfulness of my senior management team and will forever be grateful for everything they did for me over those initial days and the months to follow.

I realized at that point that I was going to have to call the kids at school and let them know what was going on; I did not want a parent at school pickup time to say something to them without them knowing what was happening. I rang Kaitlyn's school first and they got her out of class to come to the phone. I told her a lie that day—I did not know if David was truly going to be okay, but I was praying that he would be—I told her that Daddy was okay, but his injuries were a lot worse than the Adelaide accident and he was going to be in hospital for a while. I told her I loved her and that I would call her later. I then rang Joshua's school and repeated the process. I assured him that Gran and Grandad would take good care of him and his sister. Peter and Prue were also making arrangements for their kids, as we all knew it was going to be a while before we knew the extent of David's injuries and hopeful recovery.

Pete posted another update to Facebook at 2:18pm which read:
   Just met doctors and saw David
   Still not out of the woods!
   Broken legs, pelvis, wrist and ribs!

> Collapsed lungs
> In induced coma and machines breathing for him
> Two breaks in spine…hopefully not affecting spinal cord
> Large facial lacerations! And lacerations of legs
> All over news!
> Keep David Paton, Kylie Paton, kids and family in thoughts and prayers
> Please avoid ringing Kylie at this stage…
> Texts are fine!

We spent the next few hours in the ICU waiting room as they ran more tests and took more scans. As we were sitting there, answering the many messages from friends and family, Prue gasped and pointed at the TV. The 4:30pm news was on and David's face was on the screen! The media had finally found out his identity and decided that it was their right to plaster his face and name all over national TV, including pictures of him being taken off the helicopter at the hospital! I was in shock—and then I was furious! How dare they invade our privacy like that!

Pete, Prue, and I immediately thought of our kids and all the kids that David knew. We started making frantic phone calls to the people looking after our kids, asking that they not let the kids watch any TV when they got home. This invasion of privacy actually upset me more than everything else that I had gone through that day. I was gutted that our lives were now out there for all to see. It was bad enough having to use social media to update our family and friends without the media seeing this as a nice juicy bone to fill their news broadcast!

I was able to go back and see David briefly once they had him settled in the ICU. I barely recognized my husband under the assortment of tubes and things. They were putting in a central line to administer his medications and he had drainage tubes coming out of both sides of his chest. He had a tube in his throat and machines breathing for him. There was a feeding tube in his nose and a brace on his neck. I stayed with David until they told me they were taking him off for more scans.

I sat in the waiting room and the hours ticked by. Around 7pm my phone rang, and some guy wanted to talk to me about David. I had missed his name and thought he was a reporter and was quite rude to him. It turned out he was one of the surgeons and he needed to talk to me about the surgery that they were about to perform on David; he needed me to sign the release papers so that they could operate. He came and met me in the ICU waiting room and I apologised. He explained the surgery and advised that the plastic surgeon was also going to be in the operating room to see what he could do about the massive lacerations to David's face, hand, and knee. I signed the release papers and continued to pray.

Pete posted the next two updates:
> 7:11pm
> Kylie Paton has asked if any media try to contact any of you in regards to the accident, etc. that you give no information and ask them to respect the privacy of David Paton and his family during this time.

> 7:16pm
> Medical Update:
> Tonight going into surgery to put in a line to keep his
>   obs stable!
> Need surgery (maybe tonight) to repair multiple fractures
> Will send update tomorrow!
> Keep those prayers going…Still a long way to go and then
>   a big recovery period!

There was nothing more we could do at the hospital as I knew David would be in surgery for a while, so Jason (one of our friends who lives in Melbourne and had dropped by after work) said he would drop me at the hotel; Pete and Prue headed home to hug their kids and get some much needed rest.

I got to the hotel near the hospital and checked in to the two-bedroom apartment that Ange had organised for me. I could have kissed her at that point. I needed a shower and some sleep. The shower I would achieve—the sleep not so much!

I posted the next message at 10:53pm:
> Hi everyone, thank you so much for your love, support, and prayers. David is in surgery at the moment with the amazing medical team working on him to repair some of his many injuries. I thank you all for your offers of assistance and will be sure to take up some of them over the coming weeks as we tackle the long road to recovery. We will post an update in the morning once we know how he has come through the night. xx Kylie

It was not long afterwards that a friend reached out to see if there was anything he could do to help. Unfortunately for him, he worked for the organization that first put the accident details online, prior to the police even notifying me. I was still seething about it and he spent the next hour talking me off the ledge of my ferocious anger. Whilst I was still unhappy with the media and their total disregard for families of victims, I had calmed down.

I tried to get some sleep, but only managed a couple of hours before waking up with a start—it was almost 4am on Tuesday, 22nd March, and I hadn't gotten a call from the hospital yet. Given David had gone into surgery at about 8pm I was suitably worried. I rang ICU and was told that he came out of surgery at about 12:30am and was resting comfortably and that I could come in whenever I wanted to. I clearly wasn't going to get anymore sleep so I got up, messaged David's mum the update, had a shower, and headed back to the hospital.

David looked awful. He was bruised and swollen, with tubes everywhere. There was a plaster cast on his right wrist and bandages all over him. They had attached an X frame to his pelvis to hold it all together and he had a lovely tent effect happening over his privates. The plastic surgeon had stitched his face, hand, and knee; cleaned all the other grazes and lacerations; and bandaged both of his legs to prevent infection. I pulled a chair over beside the bed and sat down.

I posted the next update at 5:07am:
> Hi all. Surgery went well. He is still heavily sedated and still has machines breathing for him. I will know more later in the morning once I have spoken to the doctors. Thank you again for all your prayers and support. Kylie xx

About 7am I headed back to the hotel to have some breakfast during the shift change as they preferred family to leave whilst they did what needed to be done. It was good to get some fresh air and stretch my legs. I spoke to David's parents, who said that they would head in about 10am to see him.

After forcing some breakfast down, I headed back to the hospital and waited for David's parents to arrive. David was still unresponsive, but they were hoping to lower the sedatives over the morning and see how he responded.

David's parents arrived mid-morning and I took them in to see him. His mum broke down and was getting terribly upset. Unfortunately, even though David was still heavily sedated he could hear what was going on and was getting quite distressed—as was evident from his heart rate and other vitals showing on the monitors at the head of his bed. The nurse asked me to take his parents out until they had composed themselves. While they were calming themselves down, I went back in to talk to the social worker who had arrived.

The social worker was amazed at how calm I was, and I said, "That is the Holy Spirit, not me." I said, "We have hundreds of people praying for us and David is in the best place and getting the best care possible, so there is no point in me being hysterical." She asked if I had any concerns and I told her my biggest concern was the head injury. The body can be put back together, but his mental state was what concerned me the most. That was what nearly destroyed our family after his first accident, and it was my biggest concern once he woke up from this one. I explained to the social worker that David had suffered from PTSD and severe depression since his first serious accident in January 2011. She thanked me for being so honest with her and advised that she would make sure that my concerns were addressed as part of his care.

The social worker spent about an hour with David's parents; his mum was doing much better after that. It would have to be one of the hardest things as a mum to have to stand aside while your son's wife deals with his care, when all you want to do is take over. I was so grateful for the social worker taking the time to talk with his mum as I was not in a condition to have that conversation. It was great to be in a hospital where the whole family was cared for, not just the patient.

David was then taken off for some more scans; David's parents headed home, and Pete and Prue went to get some food with me. I spent the next few hours in the ICU waiting room with Pete and Prue until we were allowed to go back in and sit with David. They had started to reduce his sedative medication and he was able to communicate with us by scrunching up his face or poking his tongue out a fraction around the tubes in his throat. He also started to breathe on his own with the machine assisting him, rather than doing all the work for him. That was a big win.

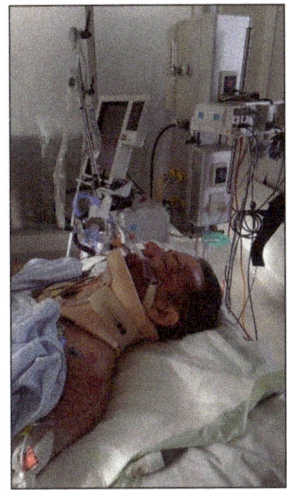 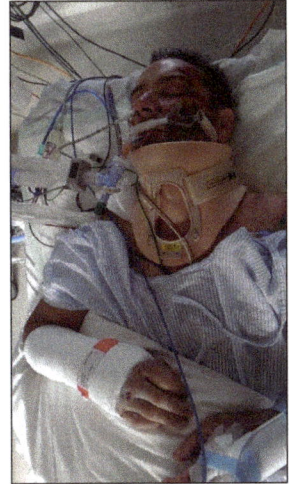 

Photos from the hospital after David's second accident.

David was only conscious for short periods at a time and spent most of the day sleeping. As the day wore on, they kept him awake for longer periods of time. The biggest fear was that, as he became more alert, he would try to pull the tubes out of his throat and nose. I prayed that he would stay calm and not touch the tubes. He had this amazing peace about him as he started to become more aware of his surroundings and did not touch the tubes at all.

My sister Tan came in that evening after work to sit with me for a while. She was quite shocked by the state David was in, but held it together admirably. She was incredibly happy to see him awake and communicating in his own way. Once Tan, Pete, and Prue had left, I just sat with David as they continued to reduce the sedative medications and monitor his breathing. They were hoping to be able to remove the breathing tubes later that evening once he was more alert. A few hours later they decided that they were going to try taking the tubes out and see if he continued to breathe on his own without his lungs collapsing again. The tubes came out and I was allowed to feed him some ice chips, which he devoured. It was now late on Tuesday night and he had not eaten since Sunday evening.

I do not think ice ever tasted as good as it did to him in that moment. Once we got him comfortable, I headed back to the hotel to try and answer some of the many messages we had received, and then get some sleep.

I posted this update at 9:53pm:
> He has stabilised today and been communicating non-verbally with us. He is now breathing on his own which is a massive relief. Having MRIs tomorrow to better determine the extent of his neck fracture and knee injury. Thank you again for all your love and messages; they are greatly appreciated.
> xx Kylie

As I stood in the shower, I finally let the tears come. I was exhausted and I did not know how I was going to answer all the messages of support and love, let alone answer all the questions. I just did not know what to do. As I stood there with the warm water cascading down my back, the Holy Spirit whispered to me, Set up a Facebook page. I laughed and thought, Are you crazy? I would not have the faintest idea how to set up a Facebook page. That quiet, still voice repeated itself again and I thought, Okay, I will. I got out of the shower and messaged Pete to see if he knew how to set up a page. He said he would help me figure it out tomorrow. With that sorted, I fell into bed for a few hours of shut-eye.

CHAPTER 7

The Trauma Ward and Angels

David looked better the next morning. It was hard to believe it had only been two days since the accident. It felt like a lifetime. He was breathing well on his own and taking fluids orally. The physiotherapist came in to make sure David was breathing the right way to prevent his lungs from collapsing again—which was one of their biggest concerns. The physiotherapist told me I should write a journal for David, so that one day when he was ready and wanted to know what went on, he would be able to sit down and read it. This seemed like a good idea for both of us, so I went downstairs to the newsagents and bought a notebook and a pen to do just that. Little did I know at the time that that journal and the daily Facebook posts would one day end up being the basis for this book!

There were more scans that day: Ultrasounds on his legs, MRIs on his neck and right knee, and x-rays on his chest. The doctors advised that David had 14 broken ribs—9 on his left-hand side and 5 on his right-hand side. Given we only have 24 ribs, that is a lot of broken ones. Pete arrived in the early afternoon and helped me set up the Facebook page that the Holy Spirit had told me to start. We muddled our way through and before we knew it 'Dave's Page' had been created.[1] I posted the first message to the page on Wednesday, 23rd March 2016 at 1:22pm.

Once David was awake, the nurses started to ask him some questions, like, "Where are you?" His reply was, "In bed!" The next few questions went the same way, and when David managed to crack a small smile, Pete and I breathed a collective sigh of relief—it was at this moment that we knew David was going to pull through! David's parents came and sat with him for a while in the afternoon until they took him off for more scans. David's sister Nik arrived whilst he was off having scans and sat with me in the ICU waiting room for the next three hours while we waited for him to come back. While we were waiting, one of the boys that had been on the ride that morning of the accident came to see me. He was a mess. He kept apologising for not being able to help David; he was lying on the road and all he could see was David trying to get up and then the 4wd driving over him. He said, "That image will haunt me for the rest of my life." I urged him to get some counselling. I know the effects of a serious trauma on both the individual and their family, and it is not worth trying to be a hero when there is help out there. I do not know if he ever got that counselling, but I pray for him—along with all the other boys that were out on that ride that fateful morning.

David finally got back to his cubicle in ICU and I took Nik in to see her brother. For those of you who have never had the misfortune to see the inside of the Intensive Care Unit at The Alfred Hospital, it is an amazing place. There are maybe 50 cubicles in the ICU, all behind a security door. David was in the severe trauma end of the ICU; each cubicle had its own computer containing all the patient's medical history, scans, and notes. Each patient had a nurse's eyes on them 24/7.

---

1 https://www.facebook.com/Dave210316/

The nursing staff there were amazing people. I remember talking to two of David's nurses and thanking them for everything they were doing to help him and one turned to me and said, "It is an honour and a privilege to do what we do. We are just putting the jigsaw back together again for you. You and David will have to do the hard work once we transfer him from here to the Trauma Ward." All the nurses that I dealt with in the ICU were wonderful. They were always upbeat and happy, even though they were dealing with patients with some terrible injuries and challenges. I will forever be indebted to each and every one of them for their part in saving my husband's life. If it was not for those nurses, surgeons, and doctors at The Alfred Hospital—along with the many, many people praying for David—I have no doubt that he would not be here with us today.

I was able to feed David some liquid food after his sister left about 7pm and he continued to answer questions when asked. I could see he was struggling with speaking and it took a lot of concentration to be able to respond when spoken to. This was heartbreaking for me to watch and must have been frustrating for him that his brain was not working like he was used to. Not long after this, our good friends Matt and Joles from Tatura arrived to visit David. I took them in to see David and they were rapt to see him looking so well. Even though David was not talking much, you could see he was really happy to see them. Matt held his hand and spoke nonsense with him for a while. Suddenly, Joles said, "The Holy Spirit wants me to pray for you, David; can I?" David nodded his head slightly and so we all stood around his bed and Joles started to pray. As she was praying, I opened my eyes and saw David's heartbeat speeding up massively. I thought, Oh no, he is going to set off his alarms. But amazingly, his alarms stayed silent even though the monitors were showing the increases in his body's vitals. Then once Joles had finished praying for David, his heartbeat slowed back to normal and he smiled. It was the most amazing experience.

Not long after that, I told David that I was going to go home to see the kids and that I would bring them back the next day to see him. I had Kaitlyn's parent/teacher interviews the next morning and wanted to be home for them. I could tell that David did not want me to go, but he just nodded his head slightly. I told him that they were hoping to move him from ICU up to the Trauma Ward tomorrow morning and we would see him then. Matt and Joles then said goodbye to him and we headed down to the cars. Joles said that she would come with me so that I was not on my own driving back. What amazing friends we have! It was after 11pm when we finally pulled into our driveway and met my dad at the door. I will forever be grateful to this amazing couple for putting their life on hold and working out the logistics to have their own five children looked after, in order to come to Melbourne and to make sure that I made it home to my children safely. Boy, was it good to be home.

After Kaitlyn's parent/teacher interviews on Thursday, 24th March 2016, the kids and I made the long drive back down to the hospital. I had spoken to the ICU en route and been advised that they would be transferring David to the Trauma Ward in the next hour or so, so we went straight to the hotel to drop off our luggage before walking over to the hospital. I had no desire for the kids to see inside the ICU—it was a confronting enough environment for an adult, let alone young children. The nurse had also informed me that David had had a rough night after I left and was in low spirits.

We arrived at the hospital in the early afternoon and headed up to the Trauma Ward where David was now located. I was informed that the MRI results were back and that they would be putting a halo brace on David; there was severe ligament damage as well as the spinal break in his neck.

David's face lit up when I brought the kids in to see him. I could see that he was putting on a brave face for the kids. He was more alert that day, and I think the magnitude of his injuries were starting to register. For such an active and fit man to find himself flat on his back and unable to move is a very confronting thing.

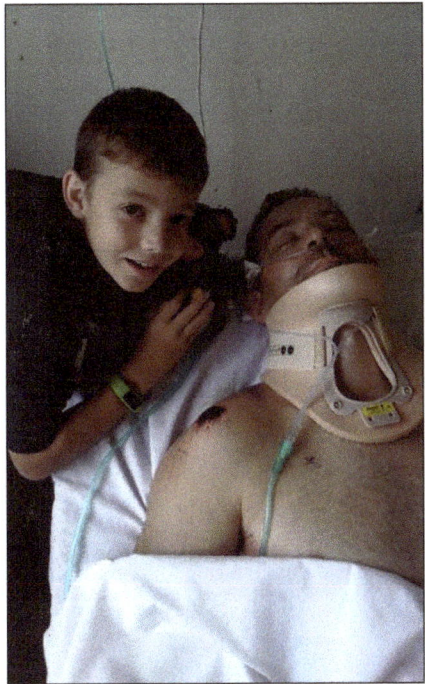 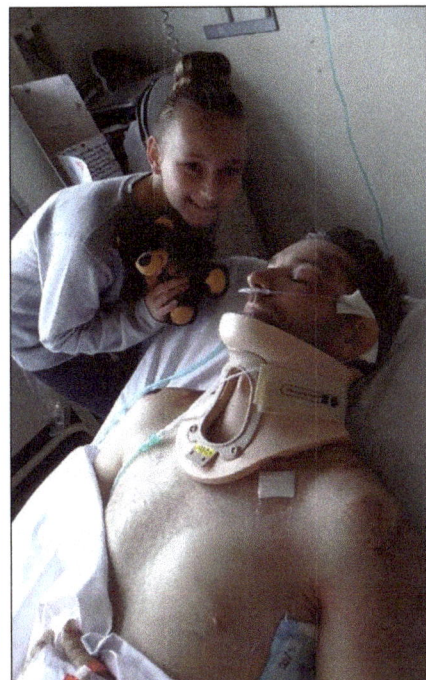

The kids visiting Daddy in the Trauma Ward

Not long after we had arrived Pete and Prue arrived with their kids, and much laughter and silliness prevailed. Kaitlyn set up his footy tipping, which was a great distraction as she was not coping well at all seeing her dad's condition. David was given his first award for 'Getting out of ICU so quickly' which was proudly hung up on the wall beside his bed.

The kids and I headed back to the hotel and I got them showered and ready for bed. After putting Joshua into bed, I went back into my bedroom to check on Kaitlyn, who had just finished her shower. She came and sat on the bed beside me and proceeded to have a meltdown. One of the boys on the bus had been saying awful things about her dad after the accident, that it was his own fault and it served him right. My heart broke into a million pieces as I sat there, holding my sobbing daughter for the next hour, wondering how kids could be so terribly cruel! I asked her why she had not told me or Gran or Grandad what was happening, and she said she did not want to add any more stress to us as we were already dealing with enough.

I told her that the boy would forget all about it by the time school holidays were over…How wrong I would be. I had to track down a way to contact his mother the first week of the next term and request that she ask her son to stop saying awful things to my daughter. His mother was horrified when she heard what he was saying and promised to deal with it immediately, which she did. It still saddens me to think that Kaitlyn went through this all on her own because she did not want to add to my burdens!

The journal I kept during this time was my way of recording my thoughts for myself, but also the daily events so that David could read the details when he was able and ready.

Journal Entry - Day 5: Good Friday, 25th March 2016

You had a bad night last night. You were in considerable pain and did not get much sleep. The kids visited you this morning before going to the movies with Auntie Tan and Uncle Anthony. You had your last drainage tube removed and were given a bed bath. You did not enjoy that at all! The nurses were very happy with you for opening your bowel; when you were not having scans or being annoyed by the nurses, you slept.

Late this afternoon they took you into the next room to insert the halo into your skull. Barb (your nurse) went with you and reported that you were an absolute trooper through the whole process.

In order to insert a halo into someone's skull, the patient needs to be awake—an absolutely awful process and one that would affect David hugely. Within minutes of him returning to his room, his mental state started to deteriorate rapidly. He did not want to see the kids, and I left to intercept them before they got back to the hospital.

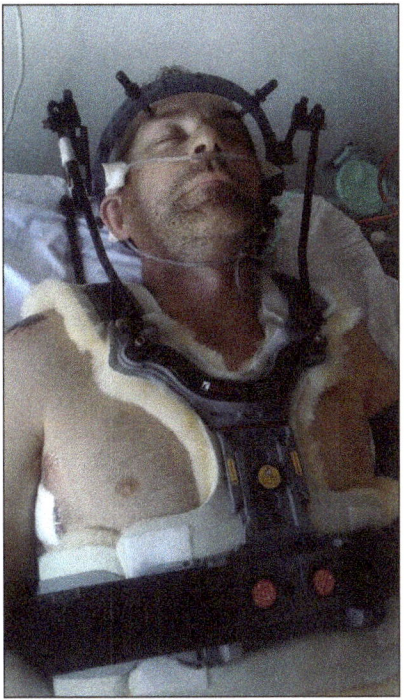

David after having the halo put on

Journal Entry — Day 6: Saturday 26th March 2016

You had a bad night last night…

You told me this morning that you must be dead. That there were no nurses and that you did not trust them, so you had stopped taking your pain meds…

It was not a good day today. The kids saw you this morning and then went shopping with Auntie Ange and Uncle Andrew.

We are $400 poorer, but the kids had a ball and are now completely outfitted for winter.

You had to wait until almost 2pm before they did the x-ray of your halo. You slept fitfully as long as I was there with you. Vicki (in the bed next to you) said you were calling out for me all night. I am glad you are getting some rest now that I am here with you.

Barb (your nurse and an amazing woman) arranged for the psych doctor to come and see you. Her words to me were, "He is not very verbose, is he?" They are going to monitor how you are over the coming days.

The spinal surgeon came to see us this afternoon to advise that unfortunately your spine has shifted—if it were to shift again, it could damage or sever your spinal cord. She put spinal surgery on the table, and you agreed instantly. Even when she advised that the risks are death or permanent paralysis, you said you want the surgery and the halo off! They are scheduling the surgery for tomorrow.

The kids arrived back from their shopping spree and Joshua took great delight in telling you about their adventures and purchases with Auntie Ange and Uncle Andrew while Kaitlyn and I walked down to get you your requested Nando's chips for dinner.

Journal Entry — Day 7: Sunday 27th March 2016

You had a really bad night last night. One of the doctors rang and left me a message requesting that I come in and see you in the morning before your surgery. You were calling for me all night again. Your buzzer was not working so Vicki would press hers and then get up and calm you down until the nurse arrived.

You were very unsettled when the kids and I arrived this morning. Once you knew I was there you settled a little. Joshua and I prayed for you and you settled into sleep.

Once your mum and dad arrived, I drove the kids to Seymour, where Dad met me and took the kids home. They were not coping very well with seeing you in your condition. I got back to the hospital to be informed that you had not actually gone into theater until 4pm so you would be a few hours yet. They would call me when you were in recovery.

CHAPTER 8

Ghosts and Friendship

Journal Entry — Day 7: Sunday 27th March 2016 (cont.)

Rich, Paula, and the kids came in to get me out of the hospital and take me out to dinner while I was waiting. We were waiting for our meals to arrive when my phone rang. There was a strange voice on the line saying, "I do not know where I am." I asked who it was and you said, "It is Dave and I do not know where I am. I am sorting mail. Where am I?" I asked again who it was and you said, "Dave." I asked if you were back on the ward and you said, "I do not know where I am." You sounded so scared. I said, "I'll be right there," and hung up.

Paula took me outside the restaurant where it was quieter so I could ring the hospital straight away to find out what was going on. I spoke with your nurse on the ward who said she would find out what was happening and call me straight back. She rang me moments later to say yes, it was you on the phone. You were asking for me in recovery, so the theatre nurse let you ring me, but did not speak to me first. It scared the living daylights out of me. You sounded so strange and so very scared. Your nurse was furious and advised me that the nurse in question would be dealt with to ensure nothing like this ever happened again. I asked, "Should I come back now?" She said, "No, enjoy your dinner, he will not be back on the ward for an hour or so yet."

Paula and I went back inside to tell Rich what had happened. He said that I'd gone white as a ghost, and he thought I was going to pass out. We finished our dinner and then they walked me back to the hospital. We are so blessed by the amazing friends we have in our life, my love.

Your first words to me when you came back from surgery were, "Go away, I am working!" You were quite disoriented for a while. You wanted chocolate and a Coke! You told me you were not sure where you were. You believe you had died. I told you that would not surprise me, given the extent of your injuries. I prayed for you again. We then had a really good conversation about your time in the hospital. You could not believe you had been there for seven days. I told you that God obviously has a big plan for you, and you need to spend this time communing with Him. The devil has tried to kill you twice and twice God has saved you. You could not grasp that you could still be alive after what you had been through. You said, "I need to get back on the bike, but I do not think that I can." I told you that I have claimed complete healing for you in mind, body, and spirit, that your PTSD and depression are healed and that you need to start claiming it too. I told you to ask God what it is He wants you to do. I prayed for a peaceful, restorative, and healing sleep for you. I have hope again. I love you.

Journal Entry — Day 8: Monday 28th March 2016

You had a really good night last night. No more dreams or delusions. You are much happier this morning and talking. You went for an x-ray on your neck to make sure the hardware they inserted last night is in the right position. The orthopedic doctors said it all went well. You only wanted chocolate and Coke again, so even though last night you promised me you would drink your protein drinks you have not. ☹

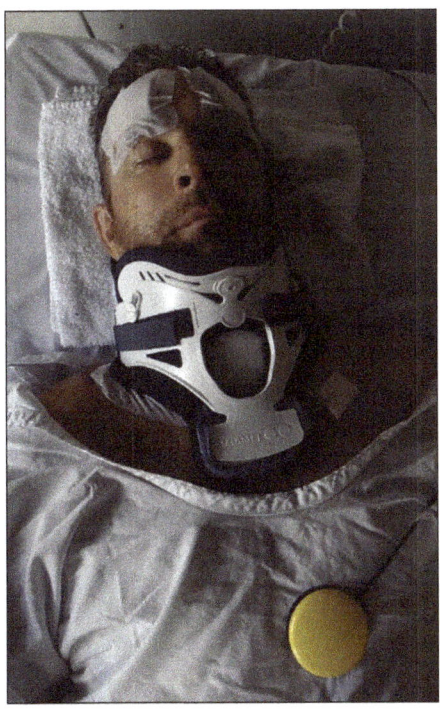

Recovering, free of the halo!

Your mum and dad came in and sat with you for a while. The nurses changed all the dressings on your legs. They look a lot better today.

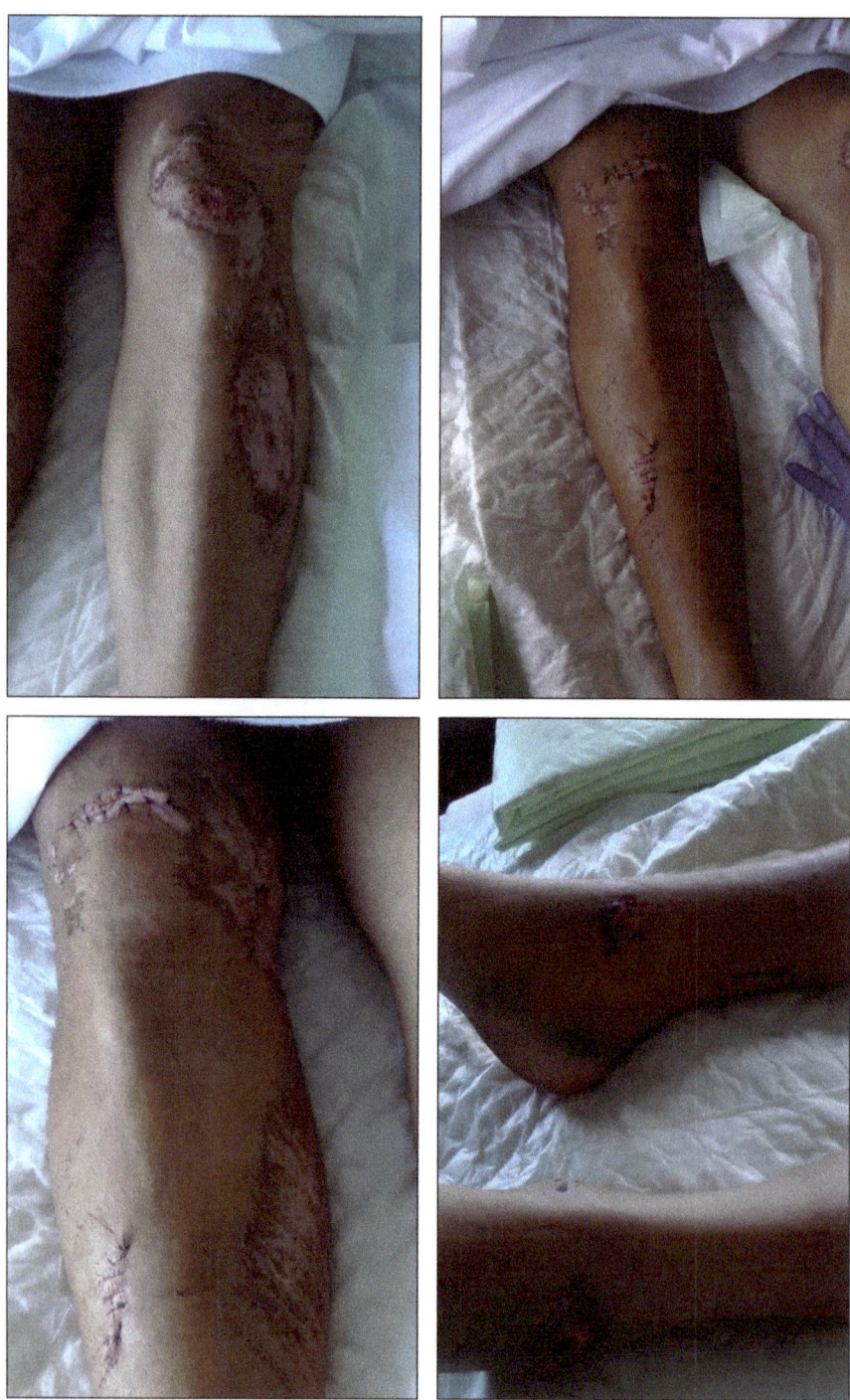

The second orthopedic team came around and advised you are still scheduled for your knee surgery on Wednesday.

Laurie and Kerryn came in to visit us as well as Nik. You enjoyed your visit with them.

Paula came back in and sat with us for a few hours. We really do have amazing friends.

The spinal surgeon popped in this afternoon to say hi and commented on how good you looked without the scaffolding. You liked that!

You are resting comfortably now while I sit and write today's journal entry.

Kaitlyn set up FaceTime at home so we video chatted with the kids today. I think you enjoyed this; I know the kids did.

You managed to eat dinner tonight, which was a relief. You have been having a lot of problems with eating. Tonight's menu was Nando's chicken paella, a few chips, and the ever-present can of Coke Zero!

I have to leave now, so I have prayed over you again for a sound night's sleep. See you in the morning. P.S. My back is killing me…the chairs in here are terrible!

Journal Entry — Day 9: Tuesday 29th March 2016

You were feeling flat today. You could not get comfortable, which frustrated you. The doctors could not make up their mind about whether or not to operate on your leg. One started talking about a halo going on later that day…you're still recovering from the trauma of having the halo on and here they were talking about putting it back on! I was not impressed at all and told them to go away and get their facts right before coming to a vulnerable patient's bedside again.

I went home today to organise Kaitlyn's winter uniform, organise the staff's wages, pay the bills etc….as life still goes on!

Spent the night at home with the kids and Electra. Our poor fur baby knows something is not right, but she does not know what. She has such a sad look on her face. We are all missing you!

You had a lot of visitors this afternoon, both family and friends

A huge thank you to the Phillip Island crew for the amazing hamper! David loves it and is very excited about the new jersey!

David received a basket of goodies from his cycling mates.

Kaitlyn is going to a friend's house tomorrow for a few days. She is not coping very well with the whole hospital thing. Joshua and I will be back tomorrow. I am really tired tonight, everything is starting to take its toll. Off for a bath and then to bed. Missing you, xx

Journal Entry — Day 10: Wednesday 30th March 2016

I spoke with Kathryn (your nurse) this morning and she advised that she would call me if they took you to surgery, as no decision has been made yet as to whether they are proceeding with it today.

I dropped Kaitlyn at her friend's house and then Joshua and I headed back to Melbourne.

We arrived at the hospital just after you came back from surgery. You were in a lot of pain but said that you felt better. We are still waiting on the surgeon's report, but considering he does the AFL footballers' knee surgeries I think you were in good hands!

Aunty Pauline came in to see you this afternoon followed by Pete, bearing gifts: cheeseburger, Krispy Kreme donuts, Coke Zero, jocks and t-shirts so we could get you out of the hospital gowns.

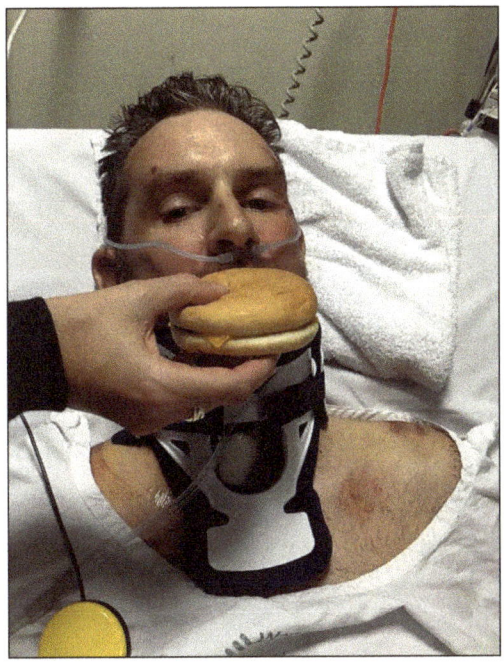

Enjoying a cheeseburger, post-surgery.

They were planning to take the stitches out of your face this evening but decided to wait until the morning. The plastic surgeon has done an amazing job; I cannot wait to see you stitches-free.

You got to watch crappy TV with your son whilst I went to the doctor's. I hit a wall today and they fitted me in to see one of the doctors, who put me on antibiotics, Ventolin, and zinc. I cannot afford to get sick and make you unwell.

It amazes me how resilient the human body really is. I had barely slept, driven I do not know how many kilometers in the previous ten days, and had to make so many decisions and have so many medical conversations it was a miracle I was still standing. As for David, I can only put his survival down to the amazing medical teams and the thousands of people who prayed for him. I could never in a million years have expected the number of people to be following the Facebook page that Pete and I set up that first crazy week in the ICU. It was so humbling to think that so many people were interested in an ordinary family from country Victoria that they took the time each day to check in on David's progress and to leave encouraging messages of support and encouragement.

Journal Entry — Day 11: Thursday 31st March 2016

You had more scans today to check for blood clots, and an x-ray on your knee.

You got a shave this morning which made you feel a lot better and we are hoping they may be able to give you a haircut before your shower tomorrow morning.

They took the stitches out of your face and hand; you are healing beautifully.

Lots of visitors today, with your mum and dad bringing in your nephew to play over in the park with Joshua to get him out of the hospital for a while. Your aunt and uncle also came in for a while.

You got to get out of bed for the first time today. Well, sort of. They slid you from your bed to the 'pink' chair (which was blue...lol) and then raised the back of the 'chair' slightly to put you in a reclining position. A 'pink' chair is a chair that can be laid flat to transfer a patient from the bed and then adjusted in small increments to let the patient recline. It is on wheels so the patient can be moved around for a change of scenery. You only lasted about 30 minutes before needing to go back to bed, exhausted.

The trauma doctor came in tonight and checked you over from top to toe, to make sure that they had not missed any injuries.

The Vanstans and Tan came in to visit you and we got you some Nando's for dinner, which you enjoyed. Tan had bought in your favourite Krispy Kreme donuts for dessert.

We should know more tomorrow about where they are going to move you for your rehabilitation.

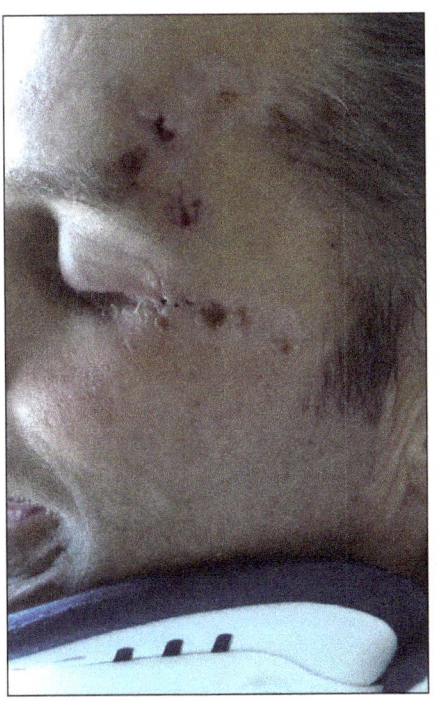 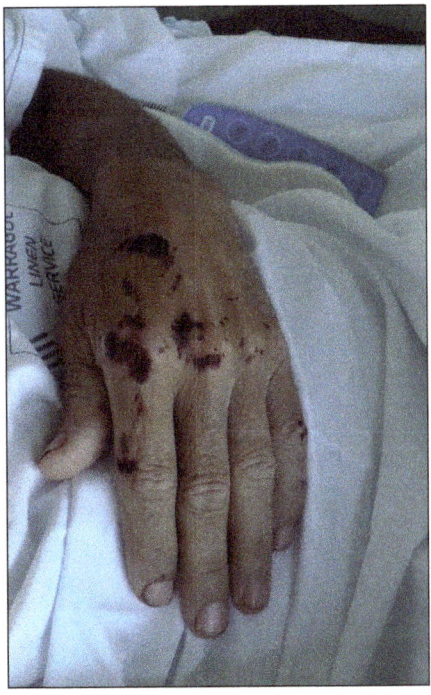

After stitches were removed from David's face and hand.

CHAPTER 9

Dead or Alive

Journal Entry — Day 12: Friday 1st April 2016

You had another good night last night. They took out your catheter, but you were unable to go to the toilet, so they put a new one in. You look very tired, but that is to be expected with all the work your body is doing to repair the massive damage it has sustained. You got to 'recline' in the 'pink' chair today which was actually pink this time...lol. You managed to last about 20 minutes snoozing in the chair before exhaustion took over again and you asked to be put back to bed.

It looks like you will be moving to the rehabilitation hospital (Epworth Camberwell) on Monday. It will be in Melbourne, unfortunately, as Shepparton will not take patients who are unable to walk. This is very disappointing, especially for the kids, but we will make it work.

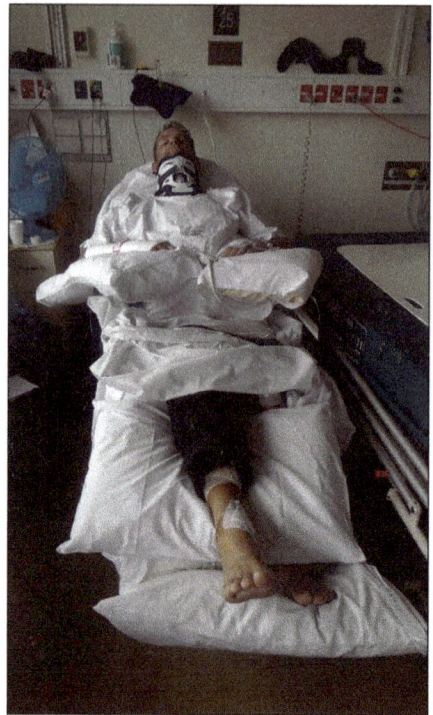 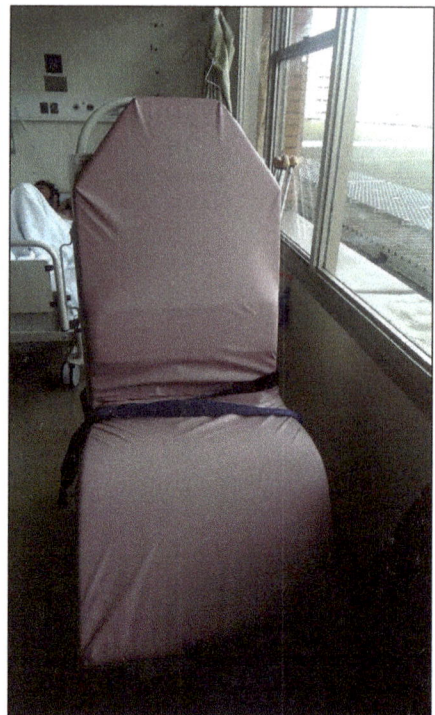

Resting in the actual 'pink' chair!

    Your aunt visited for a couple of hours today and bought you some potato cakes for lunch and one of the cycling boys then came in for a visit, which was nice.

    Cameron from the Shepparton News contacted me today to see if he could do a follow-up story on how you are going. You agreed to the interview and he is coming in at 10:30am tomorrow to see you. You asked me to contact the Amy Gillet Foundation to see if they had a cap or something you could wear during your interview to promote their great work. Kate at the Foundation was rapt to hear from me; within half an hour she was here with a cap, a cycling vest, stickers, wrist bands, and posters. She offered us their assistance and told us to please reach out if there was anything that they could do for us. What an amazing organization, helping where they can.

Your cousin came down from Mildura to visit you today and gave you a gorgeous Collingwood teddy bear and scarf, which you loved.

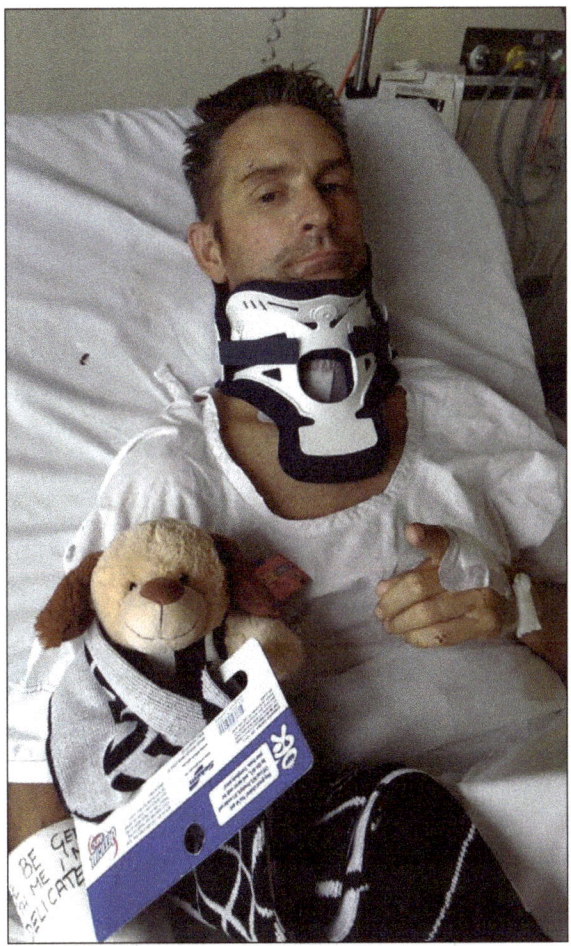

The teddy bear and scarf from cousin Catherine.

Matt and Joles drove down to see you and we had a lovely dinner together. You were happy for us to pray for you. God has been so good to us, especially in the area of your healing. You really are a miracle! You asked me to turn the TV off and put you to bed before I left tonight, which I did. Sleep tight, my love.

Journal Entry – Day 13: Saturday 2nd April 2016

You slept well last night, even though you could not get comfortable. Nurse David was feeding you your breakfast when I arrived.

It really is the small things in life that we unfortunately take for granted. If you are reading this book, take a moment to be grateful for the little things. Being able to feed yourself, brush your hair, clean your teeth, go to the toilet unassisted. These are things that most of us do every day without even thinking about them. For those people who are unable to do these things for themselves, it is an incredibly challenging place to be. To be reliant on others for your daily needs can take a massive toll on even the toughest person. I will never be able to thank the nurses and our friends for the tireless hours they spent assisting David in these basic but fundamental daily tasks.

Cameron from the Shepparton News came and did an interview with us and took some photos. It still surprises me the media attention your accident has garnered. I guess if our story can help even one person see their own journey in a more positive light then I am happy to share our struggles and our triumphs.

Kaitlyn got to spend a little time with you before heading back to Shepparton. She missed you so much, but could only cope with short visits at this time. Your sister bought Joshua in after spending the last couple of nights with his cousin, so you got to see both the kids today before Joshua headed home with his best friend for a couple of nights. You ate all your lunch today, which was awesome. The small wins add up each day.

They took you off for your first bath this afternoon. It is called the 'blue bath' and is basically a bed with sides and a drain to allow them to wash you lying down. They washed your hair and gave you a shave, leaving you lovely and clean, albeit very tired from the experience.

We both had a much-needed snooze until Pete and Patrick arrived at about 6:15pm tonight. You ate all your dinner and then Pete drew a magpie on your cast as the loser of your bet over last night's footy game. We stayed with you until about 8:30pm when you were starting to fall asleep again.

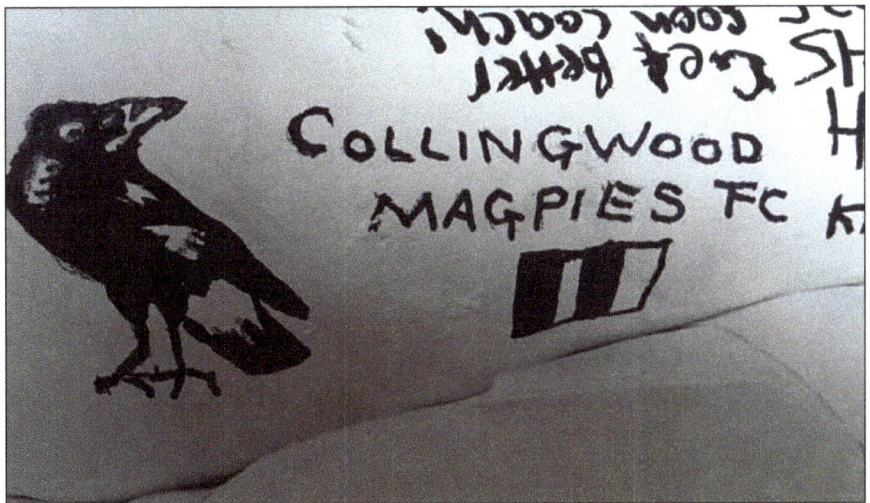

Drawing of a magpie on David's cast, courtesy of Pete losing a footy bet.

Journal Entry — Day 14: Sunday 3rd April 2016

You had a rough night last night with pain. The nurses think they have figured out which drug is giving you the sweats. Hopefully, they can change your medications.

You are not interested in food this morning and have turned down the offer of another blue bath and just had a bed bath instead. It is very taxing on you when they move you from the bed to the blue bath or the pink chair, and it requires four nurses to do it.

You are more lucid now and you are still adamant that you have signed all your surgery authorities, even though you were in a coma for the first one! You did sign your TAC documents but that is the only one, and even that was done left-handed as your right arm is in a plaster cast.

You are very tired today and simply happy to watch TV and rest. You had a good snooze while I sat with you for a couple of hours. I popped home to see the kids and Electra, wash my clothes, and grab some things you are going to need in rehab.

'Nurse Prue' was on duty tonight and fed you your dinner and then cleaned your fingernails for you (which had not come clean in your bath yesterday). You are going to owe Prue for that one, dear...

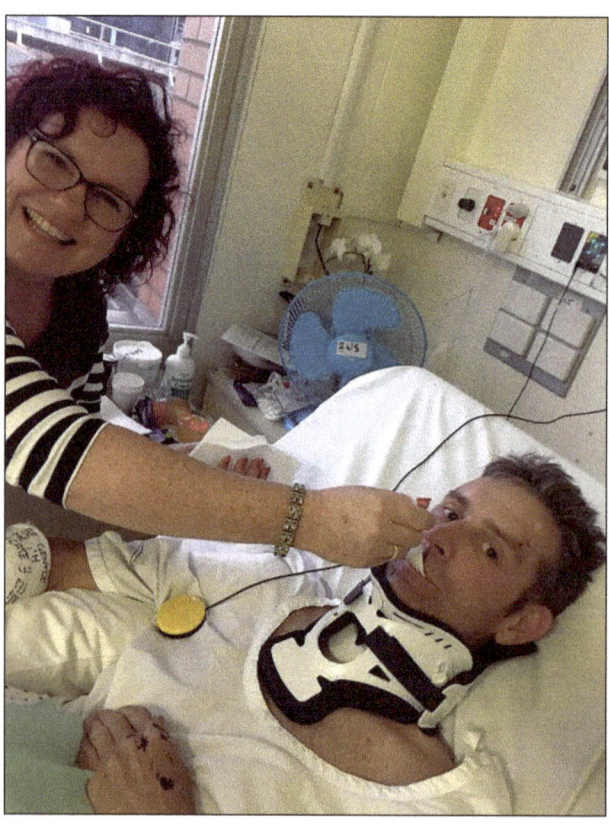

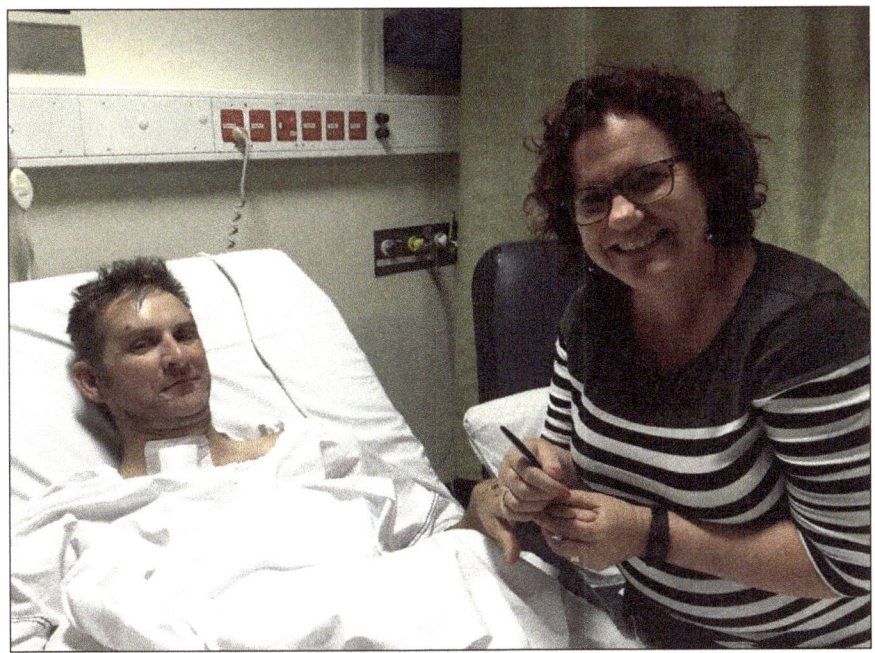

'Nurse Prue' feeding David and cleaning his fingernails 😊

Journal Entry — Day 15: Monday 4th April 2016

A long day of waiting today. You were off having scans when I arrived back at the hospital at about 11:15am. You finally came back to your room at 12:45pm, only to tell me you had not had your scans yet as they were too busy. You were in good spirits and ate most of your lunch today. The physio assistant came after lunch to do your exercises with you. You did really well but were in a lot of pain by the time you finished. It felt good to have some of your muscles moving again after 15 days of complete immobility.

They took you back down for your blood clot scans at 3pm so I went for a walk in the park across from the hospital. It was nice to get some fresh air and sunshine.

Unfortunately, by the time they completed your scans today the rehab hospital had given your bed away, so no transfer today. Better luck tomorrow.

Journal Entry — Day 16: Tuesday 5th April 2016

You went for x-rays first thing this morning, so I headed into the office for a bit to take care of some things. The hospital rang me to advise that you were going to be transferred to the Epworth rehab hospital at 1:30pm.

The Shepparton News ran their story on you in today's paper.

DAVE BEATS SECOND DICE WITH DEATH
AFTER A LIFE-THREATENING CRASH, DAVID PATON HAS NO HESITATIONS ABOUT GETTING BACK ON HIS BIKE

Shepparton News • 5 Apr 2016 • By Cameron Whiteley • www.facebook.com/Dave210316

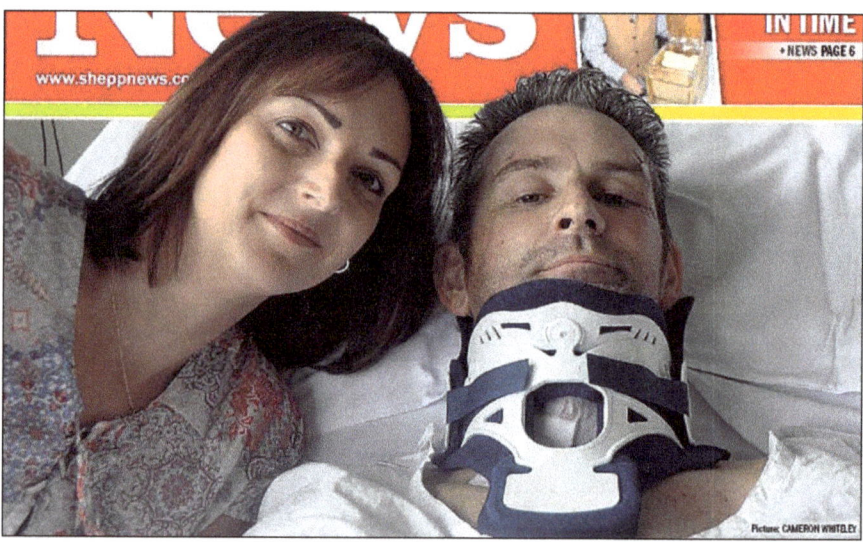

Picture: CAMERON WHITELEY

The long road to recovery is just beginning for cyclist David Paton after he survived a serious crash at Kialla two weeks ago. The Toolamba man, 45, was hit by a car after he and a group of riders took evasive action to try and avoid a dead kangaroo that was lying in the middle of the road. It is the second time he has sustained life-threatening injuries in a cycling crash, after a separate incident in 2011.

The News visited David and wife Kylie Paton at Melbourne's Alfred Hospital on Saturday where David vowed to get back on the bike when he was able.

Cyclist David Paton has stared into the face of death for the second time in five years.

The Toolamba man, 45, suffered horrific injuries after being hit by a car while on an early morning ride on Mitchell Rd, Kialla, 15 days ago.

In January 2011, David was hit by a car that sent him into a brick wall head first at 60 km/h and has left him with long-lasting injuries and deep emotional scars.

David also had a less serious accident 12 months ago, suffering broken ribs when his group struck a dog which had wandered into the middle of the road.

This time, he was on a ride with a group of friends when they took evasive action after encountering a dead kangaroo in the middle of the road that had been concealed by a dip in the road.

David was struck by a car coming in the opposite direction and was trapped underneath it for about 45 minutes, before being freed and flown to Melbourne.

He suffered a brain injury, two spinal fractures, two broken collarbones, 14 broken ribs, a shattered pelvis, broken right wrist, a right knee injury, two collapsed lungs, bleeding on the lungs, a lacerated spleen and various cuts and abrasions.

Now, after three marathon surgeries, David can only lie and wait until rehabilitation efforts ramp up in the coming weeks.

He is expected to remain in hospital for at least the next three months' but doctors are confident he will make a full recovery.

The News visited David and his wife Kylie Paton at the trauma ward of Melbourne's Alfred Hospital on Saturday, where they reflected on the life-threatening situation.

The couple said the past two weeks had taken a huge emotional toll on them and their two children, Kaitlyn, 12, and Joshua, 8.

David said while he was lucky to be alive, he was equally as unlucky to find himself in that position.

"I do not know if luck is the word. This is my third time and for two of the three, it is a case of 'I should not be here talking'," he said.

Kylie said it was a miracle that her husband was alive.

"When the police rang me and I got out to the scene, she said she thought it would be a fatality when they got the call,' she said.

"A doctor who witnessed the first accident said he thought he'd be covering a body with a sheet and he probably should not have survived."

Kylie said she believed the prayers of family and friends had helped her husband to survive.

David said he had some recollections of the most recent accident.

"I can remember getting hit by the car and being dragged, rolled or pulled by the car for a distance," he said.

"I can remember yelling and screaming 'get it off me'."

David was cared for by his fellow riders until emergency services arrived.

"It was the quick thinking of the boys that probably saved his life," Kylie said.

David was taken to Shepparton Airport and flown to Melbourne, where he was placed in an induced coma in the intensive care unit, before being brought out of the coma and transferred to the trauma ward four days later.

David said in the days after the accident, he had a number of out-of-body experiences, which he said had him convinced he was not going to make it.

"I believed I was dead," he said.

David said he knows the road to recovery will be a long and arduous one, both physically and emotionally.

"After my first accident, I have had years of depression and post-traumatic stress disorder and if anything, that has probably prepared me a bit for this," he said.

"I am a bit more aware of what I am possibly going to go through. I know the dark days are coming."

But David said he would have no hesitation getting back on the bike once he is able.

"I was never undecided. It is a part of life. It is what I do and who I am," he said.

"I will not change my mind of whether I ride or not but what will change is how I ride, and I probably will not ride that early in the morning again."

David and Kylie said the support from the Shepparton and Toolamba communities in the weeks after the crash had been phenomenal.

They also wished to thank the staff at the Alfred Hospital for their expertise and emotional support since David was admitted.

Kylie has created a Facebook page to keep people up to date with David's recovery, at @Dave210316[12]

Nurse David came to say goodbye and to wish you the best for the next stage of your recovery. The patient transfer arrived about 2pm and the process began. Upon arriving at the Epworth Camberwell, it became apparent that you were too long for the bed in the room allocated to you.

This created a mad dash to try and find an extender for the bed, as your feet hanging off the bed were causing you considerable pain on top of the pain of the move from bed to bed, and the journey in the ambulance. They ended up moving you from the single room to a double room, which had a slightly longer bed. It is still too small, so they are hoping to move you tomorrow to an extendable bed.

---

1 https://www.pressreader.com/australia/shepparton-news/20160405/281479275561127
2 https://www.facebook.com/Dave210316/

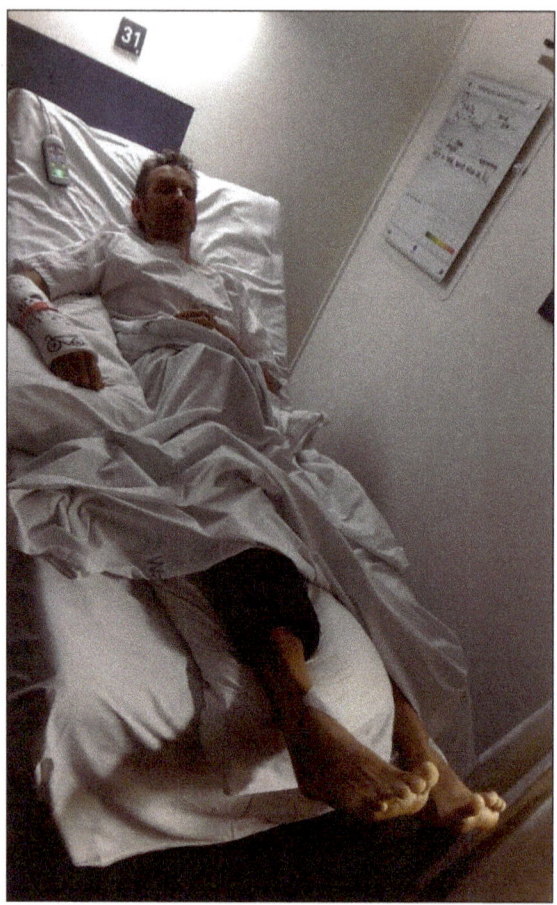

David's feet hanging off the end of the bed in the rehab hospital!

The staff are lovely and appear like they will take excellent care of you. You ate your dinner and have been promised pizza tomorrow night by your nurse Phil.

I left just after 7pm tonight to have dinner with friends. It was weird going out to dinner without you. Missed you. Good night.

CHAPTER 10

Rehab

Journal Entry — Day 17: Wednesday 6th April 2016

Tough day mentally for you today. It is so hard to be completely reliant on others for every facet of your day to day living. The move from the Alfred to the Epworth took a lot out of you and getting to know new faces and new noises in a new environment is taking its toll. There were a few issues overnight as the staff got their heads around the extent of care that you require from them. You are trying not to let on how much you are struggling with all the changes and the pain as a result of the move.

They have figured out how to extend the bed, so the towels holding your feet up have now been removed and you fit in the bed—which is a relief. You did, however, get a roommate, Bill—it has been raining and a few rooms sprang leaks and patients needed to be moved.

The physio made you put your collar back on, which you were not impressed with, but I was very relieved about. She is seeking clarification from your surgeon as to when you can have it off and when you need to wear it. You are not eating enough, which is worrying the dieticians and they are now keeping a food diary for you.

We did get a laugh out of you when the nurse brushed your teeth and you tried to spit out the toothpaste—and wore it instead.

The physio came back this afternoon to start your rehab, which was very taxing due to your very limited range of movement. I left at this point to head home to see our munchkins. It was super hard for me to leave today with you being so depressed and in so much pain. Your mum and dad came in and fed you your dinner and rang us so the kids could say goodnight to you. It is really tough for us being so far away from you! I wish there was some way that we could be there with you all of the time.

Journal Entry — Day 18: Thursday 7th April 2016

You had a good day today! Your doctor came and spoke with you at length about your treatment and rehab moving forward. The social worker also came and saw you to discuss the accident and options moving forward. She advised to hold off on engaging a lawyer just yet, but advised that you will require one down the track.

They sorted your bed out today, realizing that it was on a lean and that was why you kept sliding down it. I am very impressed with the care you are receiving at the Epworth. It is really difficult being so far away when your husband needs you, but it makes it so much easier knowing so many people are taking good care of you.

Prue was with you for lunch and then Pete came in for dinner. Apparently, you and Pete were in fine form and had the nurses very amused. Pete refused to hold your willy while you peed, so you had to figure it out for yourself. A small step forward in becoming more independent!

At moments like these as I was documenting this journey for David and the kids—and, if I am honest with myself, for me too—that I reflected on the many hard-won victories David had to achieve just to be able to do the most basic of tasks that most of us take for granted every day. Being able to scratch your nose, hold your willy to pee in the bottle, get a spoon to your mouth to feed yourself. Seemingly simple tasks; however, these simple things are mountains that had to be scaled as David tried to claw his way back to 'normal', whatever that may look like…

Pete rang so you could speak to the kids before they went to bed tonight. They are so looking forward to seeing you on Saturday.

Journal Entry — Day 19: Friday 8th April 2016

You have had a good day today! They moved you to a private room. They needed to put you in a larger room to accommodate the specialist chair that the TAC provided so that they can get you out of bed for a while each day. They are also working on getting a special shower chair to enable them to wheel you into the shower and grant one of your wishes: 'to sit in the shower!'

The severity of your injuries is requiring equipment that the hospital does not have in their 'tool kit'. You always did like to do things the hardest way possible, didn't you?!

You rang us twice today, which was great! It was good to hear so much positivity in your voice. Tan came in tonight and spent an hour and a half with you, also reporting back that you ate well today, which is crucial for your recovery. You had visits and gifts from many family and friends and we are so blessed.

We are blown away by all the love and assistance we received during that time and are very grateful to all of our family and friends for asking after us and offering help.

Journal Entry — Day 20: Saturday 9th April 2016

You had hot chips and a potato cake for lunch today, courtesy of Pete. All the nurses and other patients were jealous and wanted some too.

You burst into tears today as soon as you saw the kids. That is the first time you have really cried since the accident. I am not sure who was more excited—the kids or you—to see each other. You all enjoyed your cuddles today.

Prue stuck all your pictures on the bathroom door, so you can see them from your bed. The kids added a footy ladder and a Collingwood Number Plate. They are decorating your cast with some colour as well.

Kelvin came in to see you and was very happy to talk to you. He said all the boys were very tentative out on their bikes at the moment. We took a photo of you boys to post on your Facebook page. It still amazes me how many people are reading my daily posts on your progress!

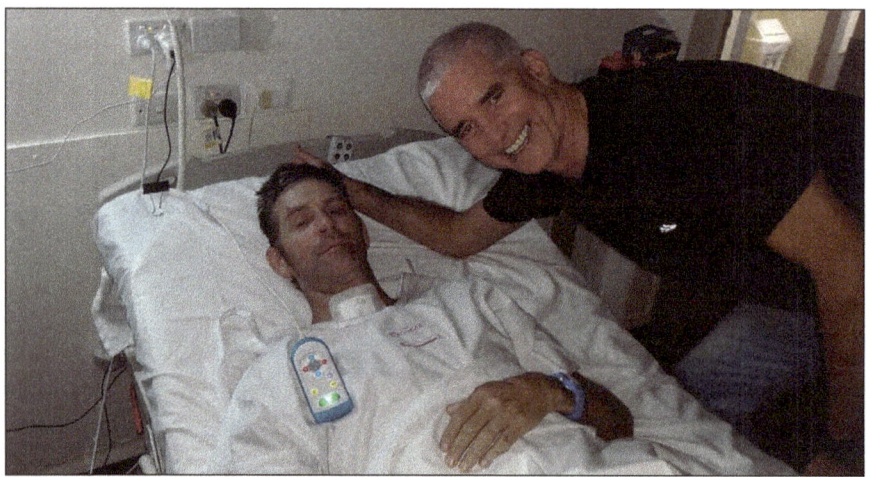

A visit from Kelvin, one of David's cycling friends.

You kicked the kids and I out at about 7pm to go to sleep. The ongoing physio, which is vital to your recovery and to prevent your joints from seizing up, is taking its toll. So much so that you did not even realise that you ate broccoli for dinner as I did not tell you it was in your curry.

Journal Entry — Day 21: Sunday 10th April 2016

Quiet day today. Kaitlyn gave you a shave this morning. She did not do too bad a job either! I finished it off for her and you felt much better after we washed your face for you.

Today I saw the TV coverage from the day of the accident. It was a little confronting, but not as bad as I thought it would be. Maybe being three weeks down the track made it easier to watch. I am still amazed at how much media coverage the story generated!

You continue to improve a little each day and are starting to be able to move your left arm a bit more—which is great progress. You are already counting down the weeks until you can move to Shepparton to finish your rehab there. We had a nice day today, but we were all very sad to have to leave you this afternoon. The kids and I headed for home at 4pm today as you were tired and wanted to have a sleep.

Journal Entry — Day 22: Monday 11th April 2016

Well, it has been three weeks since the accident. The kids went back to school today and I started back at work.

You had a good day and got an extra five degrees extension on your ankle, which is excellent news. The big fear of your leg injuries is of the calf muscles shortening—which is apparently irreversible if it happens and could then impact your ability to walk in the future.

Pete was with you; the two of you tried to video chat with me and the kids, but it didn't work. It was very funny listening to you and Pete on the phone, trying to explain to Kaitlyn how to tie her school tie as she has never worn one before. In the end she went over the road to the neighbor and he showed her how to do it.

It was really great hearing you teasing me about clocking up the kms on 'your' car with all my trips to Melbourne and back! The banter and your good spirits make it easier for me to focus on the kids and everything I need to do here.

Someone mowed the lawns today for me, which was awesome. Having an acre, it is a very time-consuming job. The kids have been really good, all things considered. Helping when asked without too many complaints. I love you and miss you xx.

Journal Entry — Day 23: Tuesday 12th April 2016

You had a good talk with the doctor today about what comes next and you seem to be coping well with what was discussed. You will be going back to the Alfred Hospital next Tuesday morning for your first follow-up appointment to check on how all your breaks are healing. The doctor advised that the cast would come off your wrist at six weeks and, if it has healed correctly, will stay off. The x-fix frame will also be removed at six weeks and the internal surgery done to finish repairing the damage. She advised that you will not be able to even look at walking for three months, but more likely five or six months. Once the x-fix frame is removed and your wrist and clavicles have healed, they will start working on your upper body strength to enable you to transfer yourself from the bed into a wheelchair. This will make a world of difference as you will be mobile once again! Whilst disappointed at the long timeframes for everything, you are focusing on the positives and aiming for the wheelchair so we can start discussing you being transferred home and finishing your rehab there. You sounded positive on the phone tonight, which is a good sign.

Journal Entry — Day 24: Wednesday 13th April 2016

An interesting and busy day today. You were in good spirits when I arrived back in Melbourne this morning. Apart from having every poo concoction under the sun poured down your throat or shoved up your bum, you still did not get any movement at the station. You ended up sending me out for a Big Mac and a chocolate shake to get things started. It appeared to be working when I was leaving to head to the office!

I was contacted today by the Seven News producer Lisa Gilbert, asking for an interview. I rang to check with you, and you said yes. Your doctor and the nurse in charge both spoke with you to ensure that you were not feeling pressured to talk to the media. The Alfred Hospital's Media Office also contacted me to make sure that we were okay with it; I advised them that we were happy for that to happen. If our story can encourage someone or point someone in need towards help, then we are happy to share it.

You are looking forward to hopefully getting a shower tomorrow morning, as they have sourced a special chair so you can be transferred and wheeled into the shower. You are very excited about this!

Journal Entry — Day 25: Thursday 14th April 2016

You were feeling very special today! You had a shower... YEAH!!! The shower bed was very narrow, and it took five nurses an hour and a half to get you showered, due to all of your injuries, but your hair is clean and you smell lovely. The nurses gave you a shave and even managed to get a t-shirt on you for your interview this afternoon. You are looking very handsome.

Kate Jones came out and interviewed you for the Seven News. It was quite distressing for me, hearing you talk so matter-of-factly about what you have gone through over the last three and a half weeks. Even though we had discussed everything you said, it was hard hearing you talk about it with complete strangers. It will be interesting to see how they slice and dice it all together for next Tuesday's news bulletin.

You were exhausted when I left you this afternoon—which is understandable after such a big day. The dietician is very concerned at the moment as you are not eating enough to give your body what it needs to heal. Even the supplements I have brought in, which the dietician has approved, do not interest you.

Journal Entry – Day 26: Friday 15th April 2016
You were tired today after all of yesterday's activities, so I headed home to the kids. Kaitlyn had a meltdown when I got home, which was hard but good. I yelled at her for being disobedient and always pushing back every time I asked her to do something. We had a good talk and she told me she was angry because you were not here. You are everything to her and she hates that you are not doing the things you promised you would do. I explained to her that being angry is only going to hurt her; that she needs to hand all of her anger, hurt, pain, and disappointment over to God or else it is going to eat her up inside. She let me pray for her and was much better once we had done that and talked a few things out.

She was upset that you remembered the accident and I explained to her that it is a good thing that you remember and can talk about it, because that will help you to heal. It took a while, but she is starting to understand a bit better. I think we will have to continue to have these talks together to help her process everything. She hates having someone else coaching their netball team and I explained to her that she needs to be grateful that the coach has rearranged their life to fill in for you while you are unable to do it. I hope I have got through to her, as it will affect her and her game if she does not let the anger go. We had good cuddles and she has gone to bed now.

You were getting up to mischief with Pete when I spoke to you tonight. Someone asked me today what your helmet looked like after the accident, so I posted a photo on Facebook of what was left of it with the comment, "For those who do not think it is cool to wear their helmet or think they do not need to do it up, please think again. This bit of plastic and foam is the only reason Dave is still alive right now!"

The remnants of David's helmet after the accident.

CHAPTER 11

M31 National Highway

Journal Entry — Day 27: Saturday 16th April 2016

It is the girls' first netball game today and in honour of their coach (you) they are wearing orange (your favourite colour) ribbons in their hair.

Kaitlyn's netball team supporting their coach, David.

We did not get away from Shepparton until about 2:30pm today and we got a message on our way down from you telling us you wanted pizza for dinner! You must be starting to feel better, but I am not sure I am liking you being able to use a phone again…

The kids were so excited to see you, but I am not sure any of us are going to stay awake very long—drooping eyelids everywhere. You had a couple of visitors today, which you really enjoyed. Visitors certainly make a positive difference, and I am so grateful for everyone that has been in to visit you to date.

The pizza place delivered to your hospital room, which was pretty awesome, as I was rather exhausted after two trips to Melbourne and working all week as well. Dinner was fantastic and afterwards Joshua curled up on the bed with you for cuddles while you boys watched the footy and Kaitlyn and I played Sequence. Life is good xx.

Journal Entry – Day 28: Sunday 17th April 2016

Not such a good day today. You did not sleep well last night and are feeling out of sorts. You do not want to drink the protein shakes, but this afternoon's nurse is having it put on your charts, so all the nursing staff know you have to have them. Hopefully down the track you will thank us for forcing you to have them. It is hard when you are constantly feeling sick to your stomach and we keep forcing you to eat, but your body needs the nutrients as it is using up so much energy trying to heal itself.

I have started thinking about the logistics of bringing you home; while they seem insurmountable, I will do everything I can to make it happen for you. Even if it means having to knock out some walls and things. I am hoping for some good news from the surgeons on Tuesday.

You enjoyed your visit from some of the boys this afternoon. Your sister, niece and nephew also came in to see you. Another friend has just messaged me to say he will swing past tomorrow to visit you as well. I miss you. See you on Tuesday.

Journal Entry — Day 29: Monday 18th April 2016

You were very tired this morning and didn't want your mum and dad to come. They said that they would not stay long but wanted to see you. You agreed and then once they arrived you did not want them to leave.

You had a shower which was lovely. I cannot believe it has already been four weeks since the accident. The time has flown and yet stood still.

You still have not used your bowels; it has been four days now! This is causing your stomach upset and not making you want to eat, which is quite concerning.

The Seven News Producer contacted me today and asked if they could run the interview next Monday night after the footy as it is amazing, and they will get a bigger audience. I said that was fine, but I requested to see it before it aired. Lisa is going to email it to me this week.

I am looking forward to seeing you tomorrow when I meet you at the Alfred for your tests. Sleep tight xx.

Journal Entry — Day 30: Tuesday 19th April 2016

Great day today! You had your chest x-ray at the Alfred, which came back clear. We had a good talk with Professor Mark, who said you can start using your arms more. I asked him about your pelvis; he took me into his office and showed me the scans. He said all the breaks at the front of your pelvis should be healed by the time they remove your x-fix frame on the 6th May. The concern is the torn sacral joint at the back of your pelvis and whether it has healed. If it has not, you will require surgery to bolt it back together. The positive outcomes were that he expects that you will be able to start bearing weight on your right leg within the next two to four weeks. This was a huge positive step in your recovery and put a huge smile on your face.

I also spoke with your speech pathologist, who advised that they are very happy with your progress and do not need to see you again unless we feel it is necessary. She explained that the fatigue you are experiencing is due to the brain injury and completely normal. She said that your brain trauma has healed very well and that your high fatigue levels are due to the brain trying to heal itself whilst still trying to maintain the rest of your body's functions and should continue to improve.

You were in good spirits this evening, which is understandable given the positive progress report we got today. It was good to see you smiling after a few low days.

The kids were very excited to hear that you are doing much better than expected. Still a long way to go, but each positive step forward is a cause for celebration.

Journal Entry — Day 31: Wednesday 20th April 2016

You are having a good day today. You were joking with your dietician when I arrived this afternoon. You did not eat your lunch again, which concerned them. They were working with you on what you would eat so that they could organise something with the chef. The attention to detail and care has been exceptional from all your caregivers at the Epworth Camberwell.

You had a shower this morning, so I gave you a shave this afternoon—you looked so handsome once I had finished. I posted a photo of you looking so good as well as one of your x-frame for all those who thought something hinky was going on under your sheet...lol.

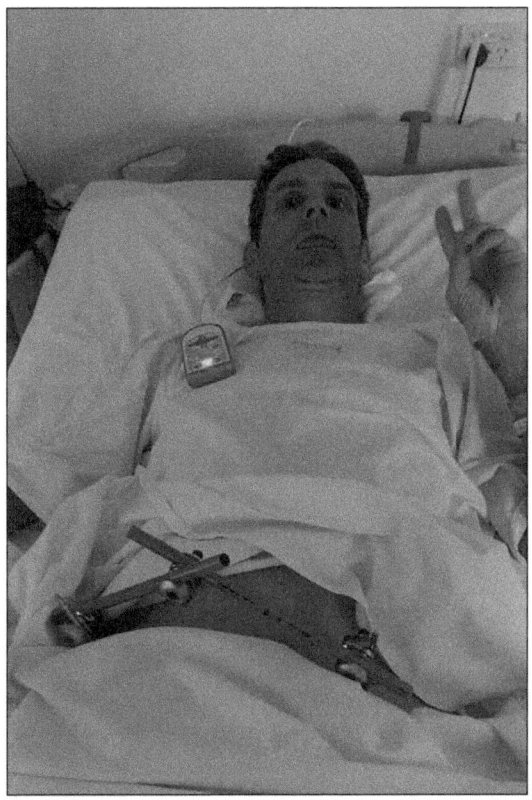

Showered, shaven, and showing off the x-frame.

I stayed about an hour and a half, but you were getting tired, so I headed home to pick up the kids. We went to the Peppermill for dinner after you told us that you finally did a massive poo. 😊 So relieved for you!

I am really tired tonight. Just feeling drained. It was awesome to get a one-armed hug from you this afternoon—I think this is what got me home safely. It might have only been a one-armed hug, but it was the best hug ever. It is definitely the little things that are so important.

Please take time to hug your loved ones and tell them just how much you love them!!

You told me they are organizing an electric wheelchair for you so it will be ready for use as soon as you are able to transfer into it. You were very excited about this. The kids were very happy to hear all the details of the good reports from yesterday. We all miss you.

Bill came down to see me and let me know he has organised a sprinkler to keep the water up to your grass seeded areas. He has also poisoned all the weeds at the lawn edges for me and mowed and whipper snipped the lawns. We really are blessed!

Journal Entry — Day 32: Thursday 21st April 2016

You were in very good spirits today. You slept for 11.5 hours last night and were caught snoring again this afternoon. Your body needs this deep, healing sleep. You spent some time in the blue chair today, which was a nice change from being stuck in your bed.

You loved the photo I sent of the huge chocolate hamper that the Toolamba Primary School had delivered to the house today. You have threatened us all that if we touch any of the chocolate we are in trouble; it is for when you get home.

You do not eat dark chocolate, so I think I am pretty safe on nabbing a couple of the treats tucked away in there. 😊

When the kids and I spoke to you this evening, your mum said you were giving the student nurse cheek this afternoon when she was trying to clean your x-fix frame. I told her to slap you for answering every question with 'fine'!

Tan arrived whilst we were talking on the phone and you complained that she did not bring Krispy Kremes with her. It is nice hearing you engaging with everyone and mucking around with them. It helps to alleviate some of the fatigue I am feeling.

I am tired tonight. All the go, go, go is starting to take its toll. I am looking forward to the long weekend this weekend for us to get to spend some extra time with you. Sleep tight, my love.

Huge chocolate hamper full of treats from the Toolamba Primary School.

Journal Entry — Day 33: Friday 22nd April 2016

Another good day today. Your physiotherapy is going well, and you are pooing like a trooper now, which is great. They have stopped your bowel medication after you went five times today! Your physio is leaving, so you are being handed over to the head physio in a week or so.

You posted the most awesome post with the worst photo of me ever! I think it was the nicest thing that you have said to me in years. You wrote, "I miss being in the safe arms of the most loving and beautiful wife a man could have." Big time brownie points for that one, babe!

Dot, Lynne, Aris, and Maxine came in to visit you tonight. Nothing like four strong Christian women praying for you!

We are looking forward to seeing you tomorrow. Joshua is very excited about spending the long weekend with you. You sounded very upbeat on the phone tonight.

Journal Entry — Day 34: Saturday 23rd April 2016

You were in very good spirits when Joshua and I arrived today. Your mum and dad were here too. You ate all your dinner and then some of Joshua's and mine.

You are getting more movement in your legs, which is awesome. It was good to see you moving your feet up and down under the blankets. You are so much more alert and engaged today, even more so than a few days ago. It is so good to see you like this.

You and Joshua have had a lovely time just chilling together, watching some TV. There was another article in the Shepparton News today. I was also able to show you the interview that Seven News will be running next Tuesday. You were happy with what they have put together.

Journal Entry — Day 35: Sunday 24th April 2016

A mixed day so far. You did not sleep well last night and are very tired this morning. You felt better after your bed bath and I gave you a shave. I am getting pretty good at shaving your face now! I asked your nurse if you were going to have any time in the Princess Chair today and if so, could we take you outside to get some fresh air? Your awesome nurse said yes, they could organise that and rallied the troops to begin the process of transferring you from your bed to the chair. Joshua and I took you out to the outdoor sitting area, where we sat for about an hour.

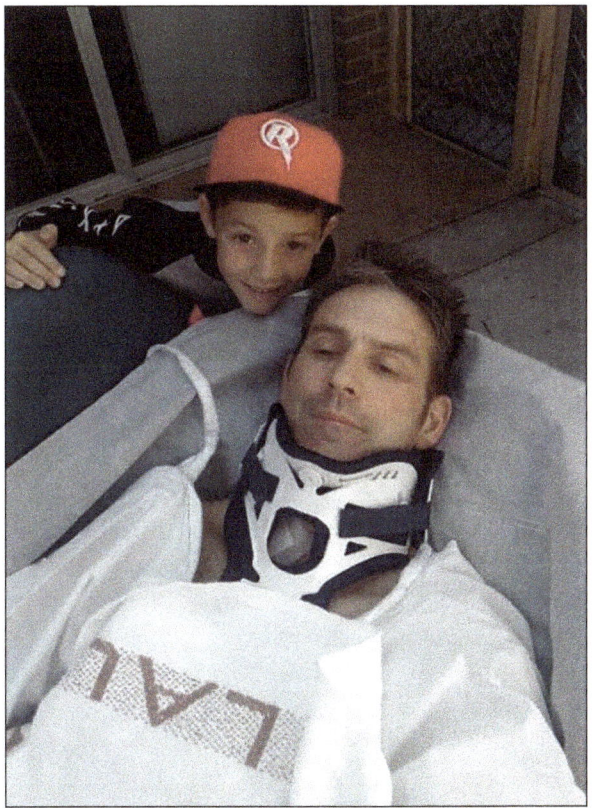

Getting some fresh air!

You ate your lunch out there and really enjoyed being outside for the first time in five weeks. You spent about another three hours in the chair in your room before they transferred you back into your bed. You were joking with your nurses about your mobility once the x-fix frame comes off in two weeks. We are all looking forward to that!

You slept for a couple of hours after that, as the whole transfer process takes it out of you; we had fish 'n' chips for *dinner together. Joshua and I prayed for a good night's rest for you before heading back to the hotel.*

Journal Entry — Day 36: Monday 25th April 2016

A good day today! You slept really well last night and were in good spirits and more alert this morning when we arrived. You had a shower and all your bed linen changed, which is a much smoother and quicker operation now as the nurses master the equipment and the transitions from bed to shower bed and back to bed again.

You had a good snooze this afternoon whilst Joshua watched movies on the laptop, before watching the first half of the Anzac Day footy game together. The Pies were finally playing well and Joshua was disgusted when we had to leave to come home at halftime. You were in very good spirits when we left, which makes it so much easier for me to leave knowing that you are in a positive frame of mind. Your nurse Phil kept popping in and joking with you over the footy and you were very happy to report that the Pies had won when we rang you to say we were home safe and good night.

Journal Entry — Day 37: Tuesday 26th April 2016

I posted on Facebook that you had a good day today; however, you were grumpy when I rang you over my lunch break as I had woken you up! You rang me back once you had woken up and were in a much better mood. Physio is progressing well, limited though it is, and they are happy with your progress. They think the doctor will be doing her rounds today, which will be good. You are counting down the days until the x-fix frame comes off.

Seven News played the interview[1] they did with us this evening.

---

1 You can view it at https://www.facebook.com/7NewsMelbourne/videos/10154200418389301/

Journal Entry — Day 38: Wednesday 27th April 2016

You had a good day today. Your physio is going really well. You enjoyed hearing about Joshua's footy training. You sent me a video tonight to post on your Facebook page of you doing your exercises, which everyone loved. You are doing really well.

Journal Entry — Day 39: Thursday 28th April 2016

A mixed day today. You really enjoyed getting several visitors.

Unfortunately, though, your doctor advised that you would not be getting your x-fix Frame off next Friday, as your appointment is with the Outpatients Clinic, not as an Inpatient! You were not impressed to hear this, as you were really looking forward to getting rid of it. Hopefully the x-rays will all be great, and they will admit you immediately or within the following few days to remove it.

You were a bit subdued tonight because of that news, but as with all the challenges we have faced, we will push through and hope for the surgery in the coming days. Kaitlyn also decided tonight that she wanted to take a day off school tomorrow and come to visit you! Argh! I spoke to her homeroom teacher, who advised that I must have her at school at 8am to do her health test before we can leave.

Journal Entry — Day 40: Friday 29th April 2016

Kaitlyn did her health test at school this morning and we arrived just before lunch. You had just finished your shower and were all nice and clean. Anthony (Cranky) came in for a visit and you guys happily talked bikes whilst Angie did your physio session. She is very impressed with the rate at which your movement is returning. Nik and the kids came in but did not really get to talk to you, as you and Cranky were on a roll for over an hour! Cranky was very impressed with how they moved you with the *hover mat into your chair. Once they all left, we took you around to the occupational therapy room for a change of scenery. You lasted about five minutes and fell asleep. You woke up an hour later and wanted to get back into bed.*

They took another lot of stiches out, so only one more lot to go.

Journal Entry — Day 41: Saturday 30th April 2016

You were not at your best today. You were tired when we arrived. Your nurse keeps telling you that you need to shave; she says you look ten years younger shaved, to which you replied, "What, I look 16?!" You enjoyed your visitors this afternoon. Megan, Nick, and Mikayla came in and you and Nick had a nice long chat. The steady stream of visitors is such a blessing as they help to take your mind off your frustration of things not moving as quickly as you would like.

Dotty came in late this afternoon and then the kids and I took her out to dinner. Dot and I then sat up watching Ghost at the hotel whilst you were watching The Terminator at the hospital.

It was really nice to spend an evening with a treasured girlfriend and try and forget about the present challenges. It was so important for our family to take time to just 'be' when going through such trauma. In situations like ours, and many others, it is so easy to get caught up in the drama and the go, go, go—and forget to enjoy the moment and smell the roses! The guilt that you can feel is very real and can be overwhelming, but it is crucial for the caregivers/family to look after themselves or they are of no use to their injured/sick loved one.

Journal Entry — Day 42: Sunday 1st May 2016

You were in much better spirits today. You slept through the massive storms last night, which woke both the kids and me.

You had a very busy day with visitors today—so many, in fact, that you missed out on your shower. I did give you a shave though, so you will feel and look great tomorrow when you do get to shower.

Your dinner was a bit average tonight, so we ordered pizza and fish 'n' chips and had dinner with you. We did not leave until late and got home after 9pm. Two very tired children and one exhausted wife!

Journal Entry – Day 43: Monday 2nd May 2016

You got your shower today and are nice and clean again. Your physio went well and you are gaining more movement in your legs every day. You had a quiet day today with no visitors. You were very grumpy on the phone tonight. Given I had a day from hell, it did not go down too well. Lots of drama today with our work vans: flat batteries, car accidents…crappy, crappy day!!!

CHAPTER 12

Two Steps Forward, One Step Back

Journal Entry — Day 44: Tuesday 3rd May 2016

You saw your doctor today. She is very happy with your progress and does not believe that there is any nerve damage, which is fantastic! She believes that it will just be a matter of retraining your muscles in order for you to walk again, so once you are able to bear weight on them, you will be walking in no time.

You are feeling very ill in the stomach and have not been able to poo. It is making you extremely short with the kids and I when we talk to you. The kids and I had our first counseling session tonight. It went well. Both the kids liked Bob and started to open up to him about how they are feeling and coping with everything that is going on, which is really good. We are seeing him again next Tuesday.

Journal Entry — Day 45: Wednesday 4th May 2016

You are not doing so well today. You have been very sick since last night, which is really draining on you. You still cannot go to the toilet, which is making you very unhappy and leaving you in a lot of pain. You told Pete not to come in today and now he is feeling guilty for ignoring you and coming in anyway. I told him you actually enjoyed having him there, so to not feel guilty for going in.

It made such a difference that so many people took the time to go in and visit David or post messages on his page. While he couldn't read them at the time, it was amazing to have them recorded so that when he was well enough he could read through all the messages from friends, family, and even complete strangers encouraging him and wishing him a speedy recovery.

You finally managed to go to the toilet, but it has not made you feel any better. We are hoping that your doctor will be in to see you tomorrow to try and sort out what is going on. Praying you get a good night's sleep tonight and are feeling better in the morning.

Journal Entry — Day 46: Thursday 5th May 2016

You are feeling a bit better today. Still not 100%, but better than you have been. You are looking a bit pale, but that could just be your tan fading after seven weeks with no sun. The doctors came in to see you and are trying to sort out a plan of action to keep you regular.

You had some blood tests done; we are still waiting on the results. Your mum and dad were here when I arrived today. You were feeling sick again and did not want your dinner, so I ate it. 😊 *We are heading back to the Alfred tomorrow morning for x-rays on* all your broken bones to see how they are healing and to see if you can get the x-frame removed. Fingers crossed the internal healing is going as well as the external healing.

Your nurse had us laughing when you asked him for a pan, and he called out, "Clean-up in aisle 13!" as you thought you may have had an accident. He called for a mop and bucket and came back in with a broom! We had a good laugh with him over it. You need to be able to laugh at what is really a 'crappy' situation.

It is just the two of us now, having a quiet night together, which is nice.

Journal Entry — Day 47: Friday 6th May 2016

Great day today! You slept well last night and were still asleep when I arrived at 7:30am. We went to the Alfred for your x-rays and to speak to your surgeons, which took almost six hours. All your fractures are healing well, and the doctors are happy with your progress. Starting from the top of your body: your neck fracture is stable, and you no longer need to wear your neck brace when you are immobile. Once you start learning to walk again, it will have to go back on (much to your disgust), but you are relieved to have some respite from it for now. Your clavicles (collarbones) have healed well overall. Your right one has not joined up as it should have and will require surgery down the track to fix it, but they are not worried about it at present. Your right wrist is on track and they have removed the plaster cast. You will require extensive physiotherapy on it now to regain the full use and strength of it. Your pelvis appears to have healed well and you are booked in for surgery next Tuesday to have the x-fix frame removed. You are extremely excited—getting it removed will change everything. At this stage, they do not think that you are going to require further surgery on your pelvis as everything appears to have healed really well, but they will confirm this on Tuesday after the surgery. Your right knee is progressing well, and physio is to continue. All in all, an incredibly positive outcome from today's visit.

Journal Entry — Day 48: Saturday 7th May 2016

A quiet day today. You are unable to go to the toilet again, which is making you feel very unwell. An unfortunate side effect of being bedridden for almost seven weeks. It is amazing how much our bodies need movement in order to function at their best. Hopefully, your new medication will work overnight and you will feel better in the morning.

You loved hearing all about Joshua's first U10's footy game. He played really well and is feeling pretty proud of himself. It was also hard for you as you really wanted to be at his game. I think this is one of the hardest things for you as you love watching and being a part of the kid's sport. Kaitlyn is especially struggling with you not being at her netball games, coaching as you were planning to do this season. It is just not the same without Dad there!

We had a quiet afternoon with you before heading back to the hotel. See you in the morning xx.

Journal Entry — Day 49: Sunday 8th May 2016 (Mother's Day)

You had a good day today. You got your long overdue shower. I knocked your x-frame by accident whilst giving you a shave this morning and had my first meltdown since your accident. The kids are forever annoying each other and being difficult. I know it is their way of coping with all the fear and change that is happening, but it is really tough on me. I went and sat outside, crying. I am so tired of having to deal with them and everything else on my own. I never seem to get it all done. Just when I think I can sit down and relax, there is something else that needs my attention. I am starting to wonder if I can do this…

One of the hospital staff came out with a blanket and a box of tissues and said, "We were all wondering when this was going to happen! You have been so strong for the last seven weeks; you do know this needed to happen, right? Can I get you a cup of tea?" The staff are so lovely here.

Joshua came out to check on me and give me cuddles and then we came back in. Joshua had some lovely gifts for me from the Mother's Day stall at school, and you and Tan had organised a present for me from the kids. A lovely pair of Peter Alexander PJs that I cannot wait to wear. Definitely an indulgence that I would not buy for myself. (Thanks, Tan, for doing the shopping xx.)

We headed home early today as you were tired and wanted to sleep, and the kids and I were tired as well. You were very relieved to get your bowels working after we left this evening. Lovely poo updates for us by the time we got home…lol.

Thank you again to everyone for your support: from minding the kids, delivering our Sunday night care packages, mowing the lawns, doing school drop-offs and pick-ups, visiting Dave, and for caring enough to ask how the kids and I are doing when you see us. I could not do this without each and every one of you!

Journal Entry — Day 50: Monday 9th May 2016

You were in good spirits this morning. The day seems to crawl by when you're looking forward to something as exciting as getting your x-frame off tomorrow, though! Slater & Gordon Lawyers contacted you this morning and offered you a free chat with one of their TAC Compensation Specialists. You agreed and they want to meet with you in person.

You said goodbye to your physio Angie today, as she has been rostered on at another location for the next few months. Sam and you made a deal that once you are walking again you will go and visit her. Sam said you will like your new physio—which is good, because if you do not like someone you will not do anything they ask. Could make for very trying physio sessions! I certainly hope she has a good sense of humour...

I did interviews today to replace the driver we have had to let go! I so do not have time for this shit at the moment! The kids and I had our second counselling session with Bob this evening. It went well, the kids really needed it.

I told your social media audience that I will post an update tomorrow once you are out of surgery to let everyone know how you are doing. You said you will be good for visitors on Wednesday...I love your positivity! Good thing we have Facebook so I can post a retraction on the offer if you are not feeling up to it.

Journal Entry — Day 51: Tuesday 10th May 2016

The surgery went really well this afternoon, although it was a very long day for both of us. The surgery was delayed, and you have only just now arrived back at Epworth after being at the Alfred all day—it's after 6pm! The x-fix frame is off and there is no further internal fixation required, as the injuries are all healing very well based on the information we currently have.

You are very tired but starving and have just asked me to organise dinner for you, which is a great sign. So, I did a pizza run for dinner and you are feeling fine—they have you on really good painkillers and apparently are not in any pain.

Journal Entry — Day 52: Wednesday 11th May 2016

You slept well last night. Your new physio Nikki and your occupational therapist Sarah came in with a walking frame this morning. Your orthopedic surgeon has given Nikki the all-clear to get you out of bed. I reminded them that you are not allowed to bear weight on your right leg yet and have to wear your neck brace whilst up for the first week.

You sat up with Nikki's assistance, got a bit lightheaded but pushed through it, and managed to sit on the side of your bed for about five minutes. An awesome feat after just over seven weeks of lying flat on your back. You understandably needed a rest after that.

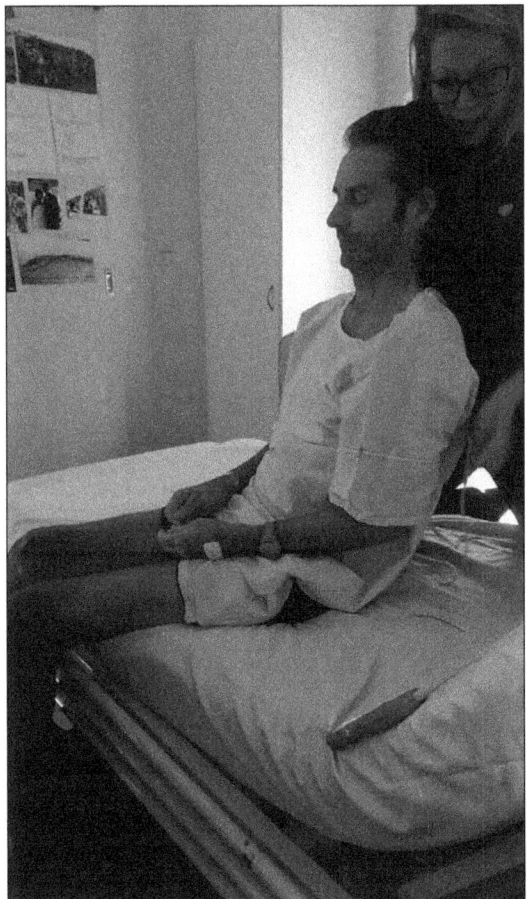

Sitting up in bed for the first time in seven weeks!

They got you into a wheelchair this afternoon and you wheeled yourself around the hospital for the first time. You locked one of the nurses in a cupboard, which you thought was hilarious! Luckily, she has a great sense of humour and was *happy to laugh along at your antics. It was nice for you to get dressed for the first time since the accident, even if it was only a pair of boxers and a t-shirt.*

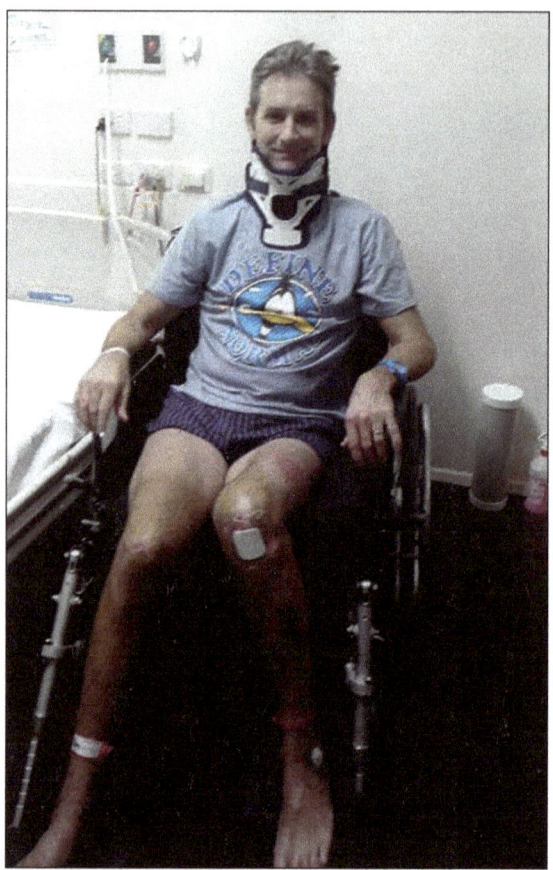

Dressed (sort of) and in a wheelchair!

They said they will keep you here until you can walk properly and only need the wheelchair for big trips. You are not too happy about this, but it has given you something to work for. You have a lot of work to do in order to retrain your muscles to walk again. They are hoping to get you up and bearing weight on your left leg within a few days. We are hoping for a June release date if you continue to improve and heal as you have been to date.

You are one very happy, but exhausted boy tonight. Lots of visitors today, as well as your first roll around the hospital, has taken its toll on you.

Journal Entry — Day 53: Thursday 12th May 2016

You are a very tired boy today after your big adventures yesterday! You only got out of bed to sit in the weighing chair today. You have lost 12kgs so far since the accident, dropping from a respectable 85.5kgs to an alarming 73.5kgs today. For a guy who is just shy of 6'4", 73.5kgs is too light. We need to get some meat back on you.

No wheelchair trips today, as you were just too tired. They are hoping to get you in the shower chair tomorrow for a proper shower and maybe even a haircut.

You reckon you lost another 2kgs this afternoon with your bowels deciding to start working again. Gravity is a wonderful thing.

You also had the head of Homesglen Nursing come out to see you after you provided feedback for them on their nursing students. Something different to break up the boredom.

Journal Entry — Day 54: Friday 13th May 2016

You got your hair cut today as well as a shave, but unfortunately, they came at a price! Your body did not appreciate being upright for that long and you started vomiting and your blood pressure plummeted. This resulted in a quick rinse to get the hair off you before being put back to bed very quickly. You recovered quickly once you were lying down again, but were very disappointed to have missed out on the nice, hot, proper shower you were hoping for.

You have started giving me orders over the phone whenever you call—which is not appreciated! I do not think you have any idea just how hard and exhausting it is to work full time, run our business (including doing interviews and preparing to have to sack an employee), put together tender documents, look after the kids and do sport runs, etc. whilst still trying to feed us, do all the washing (yours included), keep the house under control, and still come to Melbourne multiple times every week to visit you!!

Oh, and you look like a criminal with the shaved head…I hate it…lol. But I am glad that you are starting to feel like your old self again!

Journal Entry — Day 55: Saturday 14th May 2016

You had a quiet day today. You got the shower that you missed out on yesterday, which you enjoyed. You are loving the fact that you can now get yourself into your wheelchair to go to the toilet, rather than having to use bedpans. Some independence at last, even if it comes at a price—it takes a lot of energy for you to get from bed to chair and back again. It is amazing what a difference a few days and a whole lot of determination can do, though!

The kids are sad at not getting to see you this weekend, but are very excited that the boys are going to put their trampoline up for them tomorrow during the working bee that the cycling community has organised to help us out at the house. I am sure the kids will have plenty to tell Dad tomorrow night when they Skype to say goodnight.

Journal Entry — Day 56: Sunday 15th May 2016

Today the cycling community came out and had a working bee at our place, giving up their Sunday morning to do an amazing amount of work at the property. We can never thank each and every one of them for everything they did in those three hours! Everything from building fences, putting together the kids' trampoline, weeding, pruning hedges, clearing the paths of weeds and then moving 10.5m of gravel to finish the pathways, trimming edges, mowing lawns, fixing the shed door, putting in sleepers, *repairing the wheel on the lawn mower, and the list goes on! My dad cooked lunch for all the workers and then stayed on this afternoon with Mum to help me finish cleaning the outdoor furniture and the decks. The place looks amazing and it is all thanks to the efforts of the cycling community we are very proud to be a part of. A special thanks to S & D Davies Fencing for taking charge of the fence project; it looks fantastic and I am so grateful to them for helping a family that they did not even know until this morning. We are so blessed to live in a community that thinks nothing of lifting a helping hand to those down on their luck.*

I am so far past exhausted as I write today's journal entry—but also feeling truly blessed at the same time.

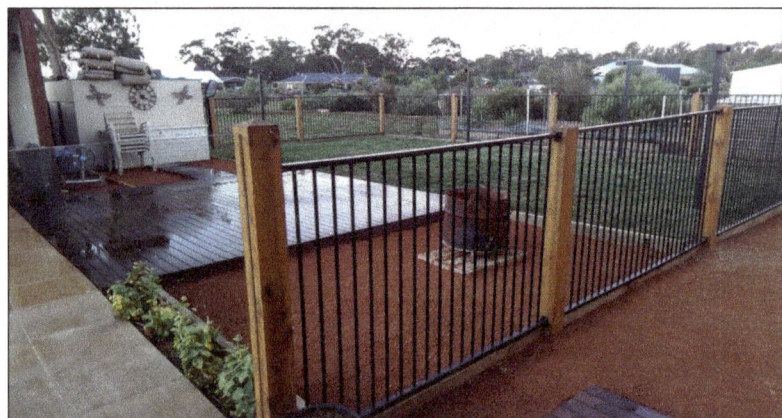

All the amazing work done by family and friends at our home! So grateful!

Journal Entry — Day 57: Monday 16th May 2016

Well, your physio kicked up a notch today: two sessions a day with both of today's sessions in the gym. You are in a world of pain, lying in bed with heat packs everywhere as your muscles protest their exertion. I am so proud of your 'can do' attitude and your amazing progress to date. Given that we were told that you would not be allowed to bear weight on your pelvis for a minimum of three months, it's incredible that you are not only sitting but you even managed to stand on your left leg today with assistance. Amazing progress in much quicker time than the doctors and specialists thought possible. We are heading back to the Alfred on Friday for more scans and, hopefully, the all-clear to start bearing weight on your right leg.

One of your nurses gave you a set of training wheels today, which we both thought was hilarious.

A gift of training wheels from a nurse with a great sense of humor.

It is amazing how quickly the nursing staff have got to know you and that they can have a joke and a laugh with you. These people are seriously awesome for the amazing care they provide to their patients and their families. I am eternally grateful to the staff at the Epworth Camberwell for everything they have done and continue to do for you.

Journal Entry — Day 58: Tuesday 17th May 2016

You had two sessions of physio again today. You are standing well on your left leg and can shower daily and get dressed. This makes a huge difference to how you are feeling.

They upgraded your wheelchair today to the 'racing' model...Lord help us and the nursing staff...lol. You are still feeling unwell all the time, which you are finding very frustrating. Hopefully, a good night's sleep will see you feeling better in the morning.

Journal Entry — Day 59: Wednesday 18th May 2016

No updates today in your journal or on Facebook for the first time since your accident! I was simply too tired and could not be bothered... ☹

Journal Entry — Day 60: Thursday 19th May 2016

You had a good day today. You are standing on one leg with relative ease and managing very well in your wheelchair, zooming around the hospital and being a pain for the nurses.

They sent you down for x-rays today as you have been having pain in your right shoulder. They discovered another broken bone at the back of your shoulder, bringing the count to 24 now—according to Joshua, who is quite fascinated at all the bones you managed to break. Not great news, but news that, upon investigation, the medical team at the Alfred were already aware of but had not bothered to mention as they planned to deal with it later. We are hopeful that they will fix this at the same time as your collarbone.

On the upside, Dr Kirily signed off on you having a day trip on Sunday. The kids are very excited about being able to take you out for lunch. Your first trip outside the hospital not in the back of an ambulance and one step closer to bringing you home.

You met Pete at the lift this afternoon, which he thought was great. Pete and I had a romantic Thai dinner for two, whilst you watched on…lol. You did not feel like eating, but we enjoyed it!

You kicked me out at 8:30pm so you could watch your TV show!!! NOT impressed!

CHAPTER 13

Learning to Walk Again

Journal Entry — Day 61: Friday 20th May 2016

Massive day today! Back to the Alfred again for scans on your pelvis. Got the awesome news that you are allowed to bear weight on both legs and start the 'learning to walk again' process as long as there is no pain. You are one very happy boy right now.

We arrived back at the Epworth and I took you downstairs to get some lunch, as we were both starving. We had just returned to your room when Nikki arrived and placed the walking frame in front of your wheelchair and told you to get up and walk! Which, of course, you did. You made it about seven metres before collapsing back into your wheelchair, all hot, sweaty, and shaking.

Nikki proceeded to take you to the gym, where she worked you hard on the parallel bars—starting to retrain the muscles to walk. I am feeling quite emotional and very grateful that I was able to be here with you for this huge milestone.

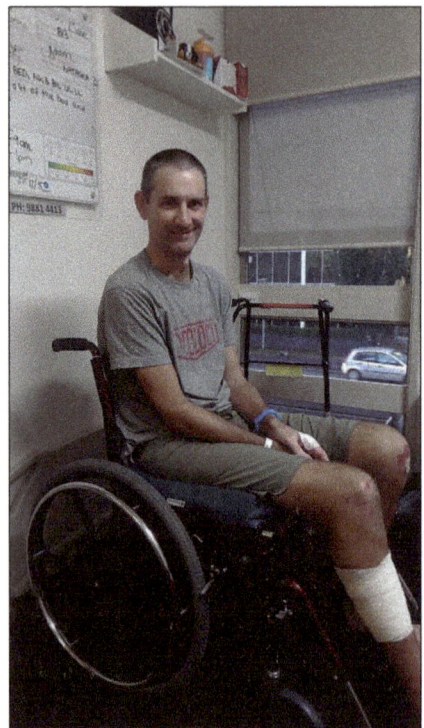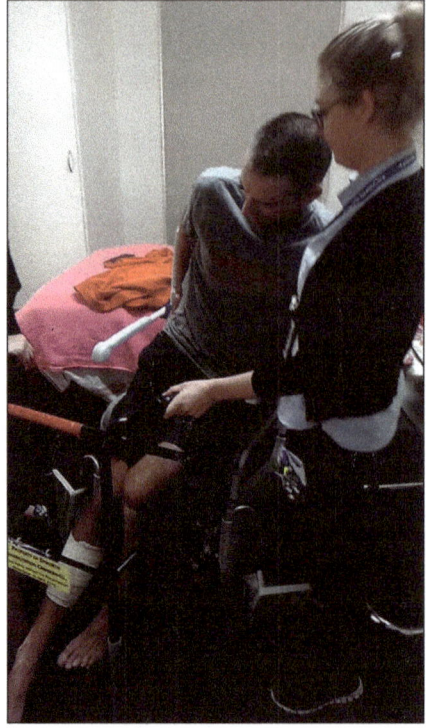

Left: David getting ready to learn how to walk again.
Right: David retraining his muscles to walk again.

Journal Entry – Day 62: Saturday 21st May 2016

You are tired today. Learning to walk again takes a lot out of you. You met the kids at the lifts in your wheelchair, which they loved. I bought in homemade lasagna for dinner, which you and Kaitlyn scarfed down.

Journal Entry – Day 63: Sunday 22nd May 2016

I helped you shower today and then we took you out for lunch. I signed you out from the hospital on day release and we headed down to Nandos at Tooronga Village. We were only out for about an hour and a half, but you seemed to enjoy it.

You loved being out of the hospital and would have loved for me to just keep driving to home! The kids loved having you with us, but I am over them fighting over who is going to push the wheelchair!

David's first trip out of the hospital since the accident.

Your present was waiting for me when we arrived home tonight. Unfortunately, it caused the mother of all fights. Kaitlyn was awful, and I even cracked it with you for telling me to pick my battles! Hello?! I have been doing that for ten damn weeks now...

I finally calmed the kids down and got them both to bed. I do not think the chair is connected correctly, but I will have to suss that out tomorrow…right now I need sleep.

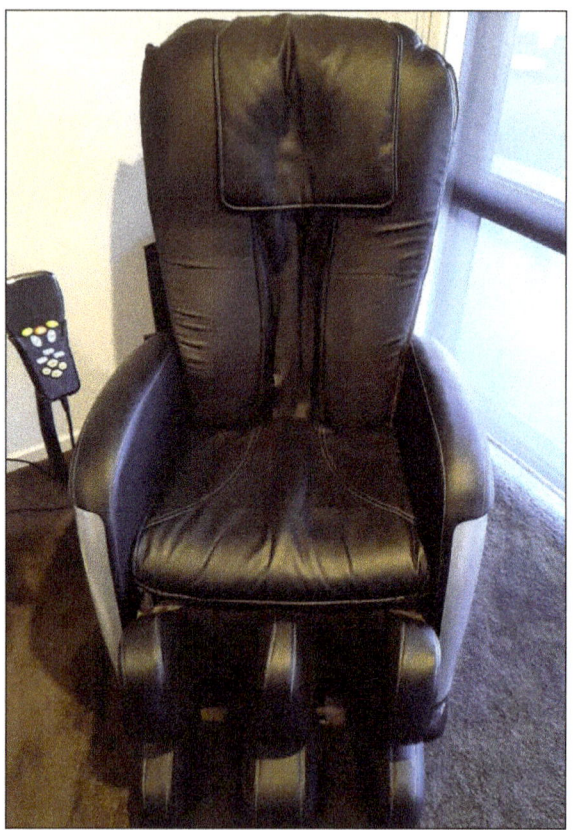

David's gift to me—a massage chair.

Journal Entry — Day 64: Monday 23rd May 2016

You had a very productive and positive day today! You walked on your crutches for the first time today. Nikki met you on your way to the gym and told you to get up and walk. She then decided that the hallway was too busy and to wait until you were in the gym. I do not think she was too excited about having to pick up 6'4" of male should you get knocked over.

Sam advised you that you would be going shopping tomorrow and making your own dinner. You are looking forward to that, as this is a huge step forward in your recovery and a key milestone you must achieve before they will consider letting you come home.

Your physio told you today that you were to stop asking the nurses for help and to do your daily showering and dressing on your own. She is an absolute legend and knows exactly what you need and how much to push you. I love that she does not take any of your crap! They have given you a claw to assist you in dressing yourself and given you the clearance to now shower and go to the toilet without assistance or supervision, which is another step forward. You are enjoying this new independence and will be home, annoying me, in no time at all at this rate.

Journal Entry — Day 65: Tuesday 24th May 2016

You had another good day today. Your occupational therapist took you shopping and then you cooked up a huge risotto for your dinner. Your mum said you thoroughly enjoyed eating it tonight. Your physio is progressing well, and you are getting stronger and a little more able-bodied every day.

We got the news we have been waiting for today. Your doctor said that you can go home next week!! You were very, very happy to hear that. We do not know which day yet, but we are all very excited that it will not be long now.

Journal Entry — Day 66: Wednesday 25th May 2016

Not much happened today. You had two physio sessions and we had your disabled parking paperwork faxed up to Shepparton Council by the hospital.

Journal Entry — Day 67: Thursday 26th May 2016

You are progressing well as you learn to walk with your crutches. You still tire easily but are managing to go a little further every day. You walked about 140 meters today. Once you are able to maneuver confidently on the crutches for small periods of time, they will give us the date that we can bring you home. This is your sole focus at present, as you desperately want to get home to us as soon as possible. You have told the kids that you will be home in time to go to the farm for the big family birthday celebrations in a couple of weeks. I am not so sure, but it is an awesome goal to be striving for.

You had your risotto for dinner again tonight and then Tan rocked up with your Krispy Kremes for dessert, so you are a happy man. I picked up your disabled parking sticker from council today. Never thought we would need one of these, but very grateful as this is the only way you will be able to get out and about, once we get you home. I cannot believe you have been down there for over three months now. Still a long road ahead, but there is light at the end of the tunnel now.

Journal Entry — Day 68: Friday 27th May 2016 (Davids First Post)
You did your first post on the Facebook page tonight:

'It has been ten weeks since the day that changed my life! Ten weeks of asking myself, why me? What did I do to deserve this? My journey is only just beginning, first with small steps then one of riding my bike again. I live every day in pain, each step tiring me for hours. Pain killers after pain killers with no end in sight. Yet I still find the most important questions I ask myself have not changed. I read this page, posts from family and friends and people I have never met, and still face the same questions. I ask, what have I done to deserve your support and encouragement? Why me? It is you that have got me out of bed each day, fought the pain to get better and find a reason to live. It is not me who has done anything great—it is all of you. Please do not stop, as I have many more dark and painful days to go. Dave'

Some questions just do not have answers to them, and this is something that we have had to learn to accept and live with to ensure that the light days triumph over the dark ones. Even now as I write this story, four and a half years post-accident, these words that David spoke so early on still bring me to tears. There were ten riders out that morning and not one of them deserved to be injured, to be scarred either physically or mentally (which every one of them is). Life throws us some cruel curve balls at times, but it is not the circumstances that define who you are, it is your reaction to the circumstances that will be the legacy that you leave behind.

Journal Entry — Day 69: Saturday 28th May 2016

You had a good day today. You had a lovely visit from Pete and Prue, complete with hamburgers for dinner. You are looking forward to watching the cycling on the TV tonight. I posted a message on the Facebook page tonight to let everyone know that you may be coming home much sooner than originally anticipated, so if anyone is planning to visit you from here on out they should message me first. We would hate for anyone to show up and find that you've gone home.

Journal Entry — Day 71: Monday 30th May 2016

You were a bit sore and tired when I saw you this afternoon. Your physio has been working you really hard in preparation for your return home. The kids are getting very excited and counting down the days until they have you home again. You look like you are starting to put some weight back on, which is great. Must be all that spaghetti bolognaise that the chef has been making for you.

Journal Entry — Day 72: Tuesday 31st May 2016

A huge day for the Paton family today. I was allowed to bring you home from the hospital to continue your rehabilitation from home. You managed the trip well and pushed through your fatigue to surprise Joshua at school and then Kaitlyn at the bus stop after school today. The looks on their faces to see their Daddy home were awesome!

With David home and much more lucid than his post-accident days in the hospital, my journal entries to him became Facebook posts to update our friends and family about his recovery at home.

And so, the next chapter in the journey begins! Probably the toughest chapter, as David is now confronted with all the things that he cannot do in his home surroundings. It is going to take some time for him to adjust to being home again and to get used to a new routine that is dependent on him continuing the program that he started in hospital. Whilst the road ahead is still a long one, it is so good to have him home.

Home again!

Journal Entry — Day 73: Wednesday 1st June 2016

Well, we have survived Day One of having David home… I think. He did really well showering and dressing himself, pretty much unaided, this morning. He is finding it a bit of a challenge not having everything done for him—which was always going to be the biggest adjustment with coming home. He loved sleeping in his own bed and waking up to hugs and kisses from the kids this morning.

Journal Entry — Day 74: Thursday 2nd June 2016

Tougher day today! David felt unwell but still pushed through to attend a party at Kaitlyn's school put on by one of her teachers to celebrate her dad's homecoming and journey so far. The class made a beautiful card, and all wrote lovely messages in it. The physio continues at home and David is already seeing progress, which is really encouraging. It frustrates him that just getting showered and dressed in the morning is enough to tire him out. He wants to do more, but his body just will not let him.

Journal Entry — Day 75: Friday 3rd June 2016

David is doing so well, all things considered. He is managing very well with getting himself showered and dressed in the morning, as long as everything is within reach for him. He had his first outing today: a trip to the doctor. We have got the whole wheelchair thing happening pretty well now. Dave is getting more mobile around the house with his crutches and walking frame. He was able to go in and kiss his son goodnight for the first time in three months. He is looking forward to going to see Joshua play footy for the first time, tomorrow morning.

Journal Entry — Day 76: Saturday 4th June 2016

Great day today—our first day together doing normal family things in three months. David loved seeing Joshua play footy for the first time. They lost, but Joshua kicked two goals in the third quarter which was awesome. Then a spot of van window shopping for the business, followed by a lovely afternoon at home. We had our first visitors at home, which was fantastic. David is getting stronger every day and more stable on his feet, which is amazing to watch. He still fatigues easily and has to make sure he does not overdo things.

Journal Entry — Day 77: Sunday 5th June 2016

David is settling back into home fairly well. There are definitely some challenges and frustrations for all of us. He is struggling with sitting for long periods of time and is missing having a bed that allowed him to recline. His biggest challenge is feeling sick most of the time, which is very draining. It has taken a few days for us to get back into a family routine of sorts. I knew it would be hard to have him home and to see his struggle day in and day out, but I did not expect it to be as hard as it is. Seeing your once vibrant and able husband struggle to do the most basic of tasks is the most heartbreaking thing to witness. His determination to walk again is inspirational and that is what I hold onto when I just want to cry for him. The kids are loving having him home and it is great watching them spend time together again.

Journal Entry — Day 78: Monday 6th June 2016

Much better day today as we think we have figured out which one of the medications has been causing David's nausea and he has stopped taking it. He has been moving around the house with only one crutch, which is an amazing achievement in only one week of being home.

Journal Entry — Day 79: Tuesday 7th June 2016

David had a good day today; he has started to get some feeling back in his right knee, which is great. His walking is improving every day and he is getting more confident. His parents arrived this afternoon with a lovely present from 'Michelle's Paint A Barrel' in Koo Wee Rup—a gorgeous original painting to mark his recovery to date.

Gorgeous original painting from David's parents.

Journal Entry — Day 81: Thursday 9th June 2016

David had a good day today. He needs to put on some weight, which is proving to be a bigger challenge than he expected it to be. He overdid it with too much walking today and is paying for it now. It is definitely a case of trial and error as to how much he can and cannot do. We are looking forward to a four-day weekend with the kids and some time to re-energize.

CHAPTER 14

Country Air is the Best Medicine

Journal Entry — Day 82: Friday 10th June 2016

Well, David survived the four-and-a-half-hour drive up to my cousin's farm in country NSW today. He was in quite a lot of pain when we arrived, but felt much better once he was set up in a comfy chair next to the fire in the fresh air. There is nothing like watching your lamb chops being carved and then cooked, ready for you to eat.

This was the trip that David had focused on being home for; he was determined to honour the promise he made to the kids to be here. To say I am very proud of my husband would be an understatement. I just hope that the fresh air, good old-fashioned country cooking, and good company will help him on his road to recovery.

Journal Entry — Day 85: Monday 13th June 2016

David had a really good weekend up at my cousin's property in country NSW. The trip there and back was a bit taxing for him, but the improvement we saw in him over the four days we were away was amazing. He is moving better and has colour back in his face. He loved getting to sit outside in the fresh air for two solid days with lots of people to chat to and plenty of good food to eat. It is so true that the simple things in life can make the biggest difference. He starts his physio sessions in Shepparton tomorrow, so we will see how that goes.

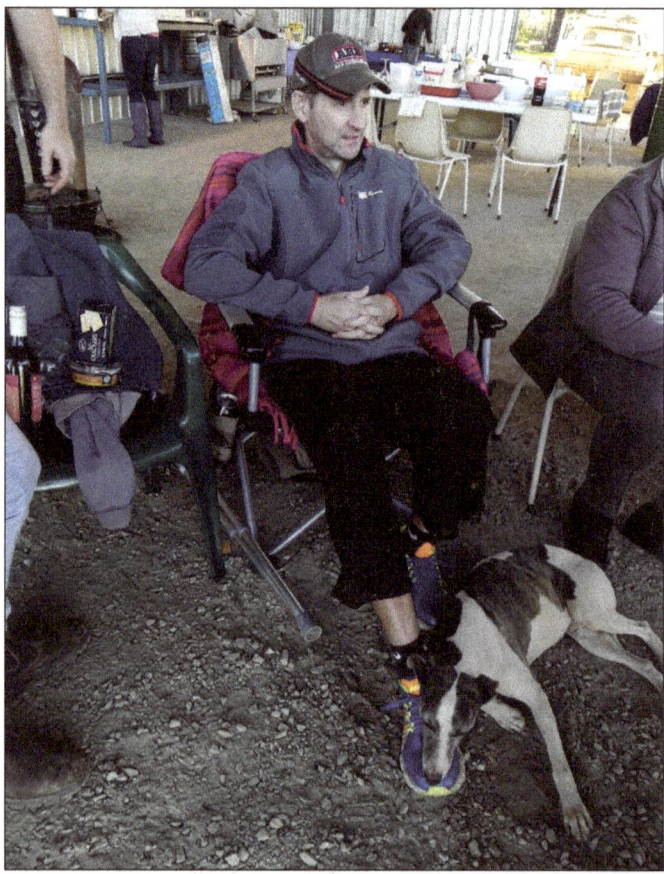

David enjoying the fresh country air.

Journal Entry — Day 86: Tuesday 14th June 2016

Well, physio started in earnest today. David did really well with the exercises he was given. He even got on a 'bike' for the first time in almost four months. I was not allowed to take a photo to share with you all, as apparently it was not a 'real' bike…lol. He is feeling a lot of pain from starting to use different muscles again. Hopefully, it will get easier as the weeks go on.

Journal Entry — Day 89: Friday 17th June 2016

We went to Melbourne to see one of David's surgeons today. David had x-rays on his spine, pelvis, collarbones, knee, and wrist. The surgeon is extremely happy with how everything is healing and has recommended against having his right collarbone surgically fixed unless it gives him pain moving forward. The surgeon said that although the surgery would be helpful, it is quite an involved operation and would likely require a bone graft from his pelvis—which is not ideal. We will have to wait and see on that one. The surgeon wants David off the crutches as soon as possible, so this is his next goal. All in all, a very good day.

Journal Entry — Day 91: Sunday 19th June 2016

Two big milestones for David yesterday: he was able to have a shower standing up and he has started to put some weight back on (1.5kgs in the last week or so). He is managing to walk around the house without his crutches, which is great progress. He still needs to use them when outside until he regains his balance and gets some more strength in his legs. His rapid progress never ceases to amaze me.

Journal Entry — Day 92: Sunday 20th June 2016

David tested his independence today, getting himself to his physio appointment by taxi to take a bit of the pressure off me. He had a good session, which included ten minutes on the exercise bike.

He still maintains that it is not a 'real' bike, but it felt good nonetheless. His new occupational therapist visited him at home this afternoon and spent about an hour and a half with him. She then went through the house, seeing what he is able to do—which is still not much at the moment, but I am sure that will change sooner rather than later. He helped a little with preparing dinner tonight, which was nice. Joshua enjoyed sitting and reading to Dad after dinner. Such a simple thing, but so important.

Journal Entry — Day 98: Sunday 26th June 2016

Sincere apologies for the lack of updates over the last week. David is progressing extremely well. He is now moving around the house without his crutches. He still requires them whenever he is away from the house, but his movement is improving every day. He is going to physio in Shepparton twice a week and was very happy when the physio did some work on the muscles in his neck on Thursday, loosening it enough that he is now able to turn his neck a little bit for the first time in over four months. Great progress. He is steadily putting weight back on and the sickness that was giving him a lot of grief has gone. When he overdoes it, he gets very sore. We are seeing his trauma doctors in just under two weeks and are hoping that they will give him the all-clear to start driving again. This will take a lot of pressure off me, even if he only feels up to driving the kilometer to school and back each day initially.

Journal Entry — Day 99: Monday 27th June 2016

David cooked dinner for Joshua and I last night. Salmon and rice—nice and simple and very yummy. It was so nice to see him in the kitchen again. I look forward to it becoming a more regular event eventually. He is finding that all his joints are stiffening up at the end of the day, which then makes it harder for him to move around. He pushes through, though, and refuses to use his crutches at home, even when he really should be. He is sleeping better and is now able to manage his daily hygiene routine unassisted.

Journal Entry — Day 103: Friday 1st July 2016

David received a lovely surprise yesterday when a parcel arrived from Greenedge with a new Orica-Greenedge jersey, a polo shirt, and a lovely note from the team. A massive thank you to Taryn from Greenedge and Peter Vanstan for their sneaky collaboration to make this surprise for David happen. He was blown away.

He is moving so much better but is certainly feeling the pain after his physio sessions as they increase in intensity. Some nights he is barely able to get out of the chair, but he pushes through, still refusing the use of his crutches.

We popped into the Epworth Camberwell today to say 'Hi' to his physio and the nurses that took such excellent care of him for the three months that he was with them. They were rapt to see him walking and really appreciated the visit. It was funny to see their reactions at how tall David is! Most of them had not seen him up on his feet, so to be walking back into the hospital that you had been wheeled out of only four and a half weeks earlier was a lovely surprise for them. We will forever be grateful for the amazing love and care that David, the kids, and I received from all the staff at the Epworth and Alfred Hospitals.

Journal Entry — Day 105: Sunday 3rd July 2016

David has done away with his crutches, which is a little bit scary for me when we are out and about. Whilst his walking is much better, his is still easily knocked off balance, which causes me a lot of stress when we are around lots of people who do not realise his current limitations. But, David being David, he just brushes it off and gets on with concentrating on getting to where he is going.

It is lovely running into friends in town and seeing the joy on their faces when they see David up and about. There have been so many people praying for David, the kids, and I—this reminds me that every new milestone we reach is not just reached by us, but by every one of you that has followed our journey to date and posted your love, prayers, uplifting comments, and encouragement on Dave's Facebook page. We are so blessed, and I am grateful every day for each, and every one of you!

Journal Entry — Day 106: Monday 4th July 2016

David had ordered a t-shirt while flat on his back in the hospital; it arrived in the mail today. I think it sums up his determination pretty well!

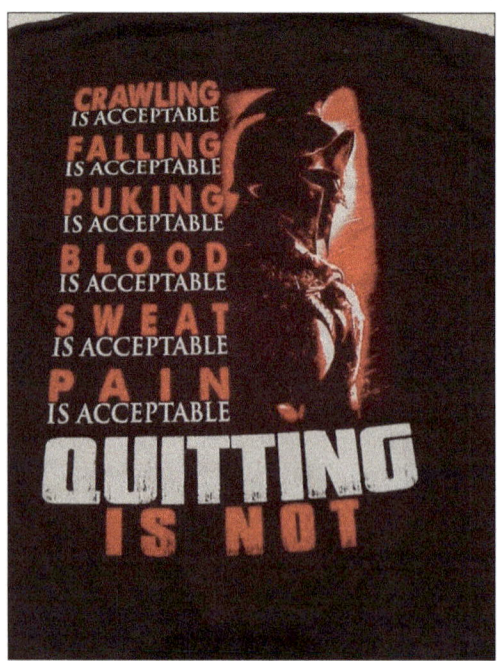

The t-shirt that David ordered whilst still flat on his back in hospital.

Journal Entry — Day 108: Wednesday 6th July 2016

Another night in a hotel bed before our visit to the Alfred Hospital tomorrow morning for more x-rays and an appointment with David's trauma surgeon. Here's hoping for more good news!

Journal Entry — Day 109: Thursday 7th July 2016

Very happy to be home after a very long day in Melbourne. David's surgeon rang in sick this morning, so we had to just sit and wait until another doctor could see us. Poor Joshua did so well, sitting there patiently for hours on end. When we were finally seen, it was more good news. The trauma doctor was rapt to see David, as she had been part of the trauma team that cared for him whilst he was in the trauma ward. She said his neck break was healing exceptionally well—if it were not for the plates in his neck, you could not tell where the spine was broken! His pelvis is still progressing well and she concurred with the orthopedic surgeon—as long as his collarbone that has not healed properly doesn't cause him pain, she would not have the surgery to try and repair it either.

She has given him the all-clear to drive from home to school, which will ease some of the pressure off me when the kids go back to school next week. He asked if he could get back on his bike, seeing as everything is healing so well. I think he surprised the poor doctor, as it is not a question that most people would ask when they are still learning to walk properly again. She said, "No!" Not until he sees his pelvic surgeon in two and a half months and he says it is okay. She explained that whilst he is healing extremely well, his pelvis has not finished healing yet; if he were to have even a minor fall, the results could be 'catastrophic' (her word, not mine!). David was not overjoyed by this but has accepted it…for now, anyway.

Journal Entry — Day 111: Saturday 9th July 2016

Another milestone reached for David! He drove up to Dawn's to get a loaf of bread for lunch. The kids were happy to report that he did not run over or into anything…lol. He said it was good to have a bit of his independence back. He is sticking close to home for now, but I am sure it will not be long before he is out and about in Shepparton on his own again. He needs to get some more strength back in his upper body to enable him to drive longer distances. It is amazing how much energy is used holding onto a steering wheel. Once again, something that we take for granted every time we decide we need to nip up to the shops or do the school run!

Enjoyed one of our favorite family times tonight: making homemade pizza for dinner. So nice having David home to do something as normal as cooking a meal together. Loved the smiles on the kids' faces.

Journal Entry — Day 114: Tuesday 12th July 2016

Visited the dentist today; miraculously, David only suffered a small chip in one of his front teeth, courtesy of the accident. Small enough that it was able to be smoothed out, not filled. Kaitlyn informed me that Daddy is driving really well, and she is happy to be in the car again with him, which is great.

David is so keen to get back on his bike—not only for the physical benefits but for his mental recovery as well. His occupational therapist is working on a solution with the TAC to see if we can get him on a trainer at home. Fingers crossed they come to the party for all our sakes! The PTSD and depression are beasts that do not care who you are or what you do, they will attack anyone at any time. David doesn't want to consider medication as an option as he does not like the side effects or want a band-aid fix, which is how he sees it. For him, exercise is the best medicine to keep it under control; not being able to get out and move is taking a big toll on him—and on us!

Journal Entry — Day 128: Tuesday 26th July 2016

David is progressing well. He is having intense physio twice a week and is seeing big improvements in his walking and general movement. He still fatigues easily; it's the worst on the days he has physio. He is starting to do small things around the house as he feels able, which is a great help to me.

Joshua is loving having Dad take him to school again and stay for reading in the mornings. I actually think David gets more enjoyment out of it than the kids, who are all very excited to have him back in the classroom.

His short-term memory is still an issue, which can be a bit challenging at times, but we are all working together to manage this. He is working hard towards being able to get back on his bike on a trainer, which I am sure will happen sooner rather than later and will be a big relief for all of us.

We are getting back into some sort of a routine as a family now. I have been able to go back into the office and we get to go to the kids' sport on the weekends as a family again. The hardest adjustment for David is being on his own for so many hours a day while I am at work and the kids are at school. Going from having visitors nearly every day to being alone was always going to be the toughest transition mentally, but he seems to be coping fairly well with this so far.

He was very excited to tell me he is starting to get a little bit of muscle tone in his thighs again. It is these small victories that keep us pushing forward each day.

Journal Entry — Day 118: Saturday 30th July 2016

We enjoyed a great meal with family and friends to celebrate David's 46th birthday and my dad's 70th birthday. I was not sure we would get to celebrate this one, so it was a very special occasion.

David celebrating his 46th birthday.

Journal Entry — Day 133: Sunday 14th August 2016

The last couple of weeks have seen David continuing with his physiotherapy. He continues to make great progress. He is much more stable on his feet and I do not worry about him falling over as much anymore. Very excited that he now has enough strength in his legs to get off the toilet, so we were finally able to lose the adaptable toilet seat, his last disability aid in the house!

He is finally back on the bike, much to his delight. It is only on the trainer in the kid's rumpus room, but this has certainly helped with his mental recovery.

Back on the trainer!

Yesterday, he and Joshua went to their first football game for the season down in Melbourne to watch the Pies and Port Melbourne in the VFL. A great milestone for my boys. They have missed their trips down to Melbourne for the footy this year.

I am so proud of how far David has come from that fateful day in March and for all the support and well wishes we continue to receive. Knowing that you are all there encouraging us makes the world of difference, so thank you!

Journal Entry – Day 139: Saturday 20th August 2016

A very happy boy tonight as David prepares to watch his beloved Pies play at Etihad for the first time this season. We arrived super early to give him time to navigate the stairs and ramps to get to the third level. He did great; now let us hope the Pies can put on a win for him!

At Etihad for the Pies game.

Journal Entry – Day 157: Tuesday 13th September 2016

David's rehabilitation has continued to go well. He is starting to get the strength back in his legs as he pushes them on the trainer and at his physio sessions. He is still unable to bend his right knee to any great extent, but keeps pushing to try and regain the movement in it. He is still experiencing a lot of pain in his shoulders and sides, and is still unable to lift anything of any serious weight. I am able to tell when his body is giving him more pain than usual—when everything stiffens up and he finds it challenging to walk any great distance—as that is the only time he uses the disabled parking bays.

He has progressed enough that we have been able to get away for a much-needed family break to Queensland for a holiday. Although, he did forget about all the new skin on his scarred legs and managed to get them sunburnt today. Hopefully, they are not too painful tomorrow.

We are back to the Alfred in October to see the surgeons again and he is really hoping for the all-clear to get back out on the bike.

Journal Entry — Day 195: Friday 21st October 2016

A day of mixed emotion as we headed back to the Alfred Hospital for David's seven-month checkup. Amazing to look at how much has happened, how far David has come in his recovery and rehabilitation, and how much we as a family have changed and adapted to the challenges that life has thrown our way.

David received an excellent report from his surgeon, who was extremely impressed with his progress. His surgeons still maintain there is no need to operate on his right collarbone that has not healed properly unless it starts to give him problems. The surgeon is very happy with how well David's pelvis is healing and advised us that his knee will take at least two years to heal, due to the severity of the injury.

He was so impressed with how far David has progressed that he has given the all-clear for David to have his future follow-ups with our family doctor at home, unless something seems not right and/or our doctor requires him to go back to Melbourne for any reason.

This also means that he is cleared for returning to riding, which is where the mixed emotions come in. Whilst I am really happy that he has progressed so far so quickly, I am still a bit apprehensive of him being back out on the bike again. I know he will not take any risks or ride in the dark or bad weather, but it will still be a tough time for the kids and I as we adjust to him being out on the road again when he feels ready to take that step.

So, more physio and rehabilitation to go but hopefully no more trips to Melbourne to see surgeons.

Feeling very blessed and grateful right now!

Journal Entry – Day 199: Tuesday 25th October 2016

Seven months after the accident that almost killed him, David is once again back on his bike. He went out yesterday and did a 20km ride for the first time since that awful day in March. Whilst my stress levels were through the roof until he made it back home safe and sound, I am incredibly proud of him for actually doing it. The amount of courage it took for him to get back out there after what he has gone through is extraordinary.

No one would have thought any less of him for not ever getting on a bike again!

Doctors will have to monitor his pelvis for the rest of his life and I am sure there will be some more hurdles to tackle as time goes on, but to see the happiness on his face after his ride counteracts the rest. Having conquered this milestone will give him the strength to continue the hard, and oft times frustrating, monotony and pain of rehabilitation for the many months yet to come.

To everyone who has been following our journey over the last seven months, thank you for your love, support, and encouragement. Know that each and every one of you are in our prayers and we wish you all the best life has to offer. To those of you battling your own challenges, stay strong and persevere, as you will overcome and be victorious.

Journal Entry – Day 225: Sunday 20th November 2016

David was able to chat with some of the Orica AIS girls at Mitchelton Winery today as they examined what was left of his bike after his crash in March.

David and Sarah Roy from GreenEdge Cycling with the remnants of David's bike after the crash.

Journal Entry — Day 271: Sunday 25th December 2016

Well, it has certainly been an interesting journey over the last nine months. As I sit here, waiting for the family to arrive for Christmas lunch and reflecting over the last year, I am so very grateful for the fact that we still have David with us.

His recovery has been nothing short of miraculous and I am grateful to everyone who has supported us over this year.

Whilst his rehab will continue into 2017, we are blessed to be able to spend this family time together. To all of you who have supported and encouraged us over the last nine months, thank you! We wish you and your families a very Merry Christmas and a safe and Happy New Year. Love, the Patons xx

Merry Christmas 2016!

Journal Entry — Day 298: Saturday 21st January 2017

Ten months to the day since David's awful cycling accident and he has just conquered Willunga Hill in the beautiful Adelaide Hills. What an amazing thing grit and determination is! Never, ever give up!

Willunga Hill in Adelaide

Journal Entry — Day 304: Friday 27th January 2017

Whilst in hospital learning to walk again, David and his best mate Peter set a goal for David to ride in the Cadel Evans People's Ride. I am happy to report that we have just arrived in Geelong, Victoria, where David will take part in the People's Ride tomorrow morning. Another goal ticked off his list. I am so proud of his determination and grit which have got him here so quickly.

Journal Entry — Day 305: Saturday 28th January 2017

So very proud of these boys today. After making a pledge to each other—whilst David was in hospital recovering from his horrific injuries—to ride in the Cadel Evans ride in Geelong in January 2017, they have done it! Only ten months and one week after the accident that almost took his life!

The tears flowed from Prue and I as our boys crossed the finish line together. True mates supporting each other in the tough times and the victories! Love you both to bits! xxx

Pete and David, completing their goal of riding together in the People's Ride ten months after David's accident.

CHAPTER 15

Creating a New 'Normal'

Journal Entry — Day 357: Tuesday 21st March 2017

What a difference a year makes! This time last year I was making the mad dash down to the Alfred Hospital in Melbourne where David had been airlifted after his near-fatal cycling accident.

For those of you who have travelled this journey with us, either in the flesh or via the Facebook page, thank you!

I sit here with mixed emotions as I reflect on the last twelve months and the challenges and triumphs it has given us. We have changed and grown as individuals and as a family, as we have each tackled the many highs and lows that have come our way.

I am so proud—not only of David and the amazing courage and determination it has taken to go from lying in a coma, broken and bleeding, to be once again whole (for the most part!) and living life—but of the kids who have, through this journey, never given up on their dad or a brighter future for us all.

So, as we move into this next phase of recovery, rehabilitation, and healing, I am grateful for the unconditional support and love we have received from you all, and for the miracle that is my family.

Journal Entry — Day 363: Monday 27th March 2017

The Shepparton News ran a follow-up article on David today, talking about his recovery and the areas that he enjoys riding around Toolamba and Tatura. He made the front page as well!

Front page article in the Shepparton News

Journal Entry — Day 490: Tuesday 1st August 2017

Well, another birthday has come around and David is doing well. He is getting stronger every day and has enjoyed some camping trips with the family and scrubbed up very nicely to attend the Anna Meares night in Shepparton a few months ago.

Photos from camping trips and a night out.

He is loving being able to see the kids play their sport every weekend and we are looking forward to the future. So, happy birthday, my love—here is to many more to come. xx

Journal Entry — Day 584: Friday 3rd November 2017 (David)

Well, I have officially been handed my Facebook page! This could lead to trouble!!!!

I have been back on the bike now for twelve months and, despite the body not enjoying much more than an hour at a time, I am getting faster every day—setting new Strava PRs that I had held for five years and even being top ten in quite a few KOMs. To those non-Strava people, this is a big deal.

I am trying to do more every day, but have to keep reminding myself of the unfortunate consequences an hour or two later if I overdo it.

Journal Entry — Day 586: Sunday 5th November 2017 (David)

Some days when riding I ask myself, "Is the pain worth it?" The back aches, the neck hurts, there is knee pain and general aches all over. Yet I feel guilty if I do not ride. Is it to help with the depression, is it the hour of peace, or just maybe to control my weight?

It is actually quite simple.

Whether it is for other people or just for myself, it is because I can!

I must also set an example for my children: no matter what life gives you, get up, brush it off, and just do it! You are the only one in the way of you!

Journal Entry — Day 590: Thursday 9th November 2017 (David)

It has been said that I need one of these...

A photo found online that shows David never lost his sense of humour at any point through his journey.

Journal Entry — Day 591: Friday 10th November 2017 (David)

Today I am riding up 10% climbs and setting 45km/hr averages on the flat. That day I first walked after the accident is still the hardest thing I have ever done. It was only 10 meters down the hallway and was a shuffle with a walking frame more than a walk, but my mind was made up! Telling me that I can't do something is just setting a challenge for me...get out of my way! Remember next time you think the world is ending that it is probably not and move on.

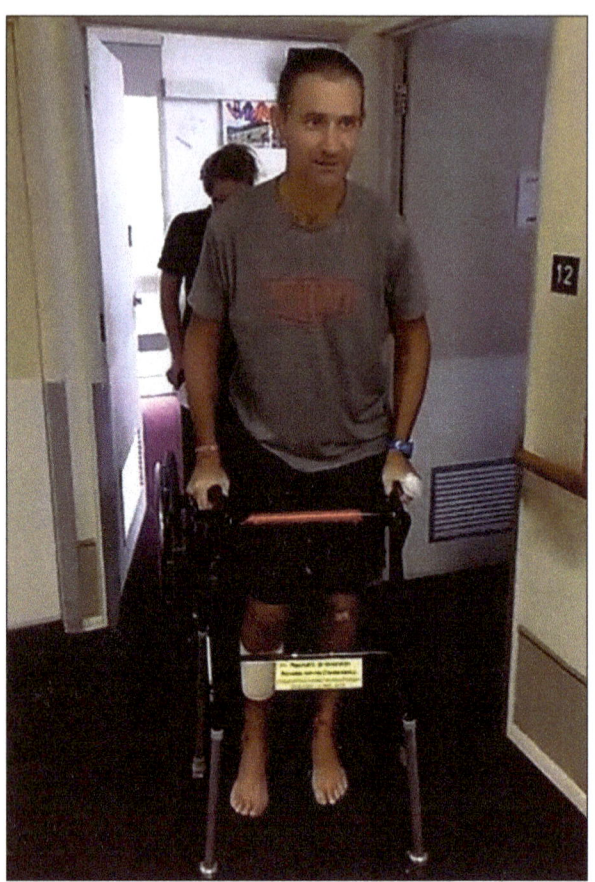

A look back at David's first steps in the hallway.
He has come such a long way since then!

Journal Entry — Day 613: Saturday 2nd December 2017 (David)

Taking a week off the bike to go on holidays. While a rest is always a good thing, it will be the first time taking one from the bike since I got back on last November! Already feeling the guilt.

Journal Entry — Day 636: Monday 25th December 2017 (David)

As I celebrate another Christmas that should not have been, my message is simple: Do not take life too seriously. Enjoy every moment, live for today, and be thankful for what you have!

This journey has been made easier by sharing it with so many of you, so I thank you.

Journal Entry — Day 657: Monday 15th January 2018 (David)

Starting to beat some pre-accident times in Adelaide. Feeling great to be almost back! Just do not ask me how I feel in an hour... ☹

Journal Entry — Day 718: Saturday 17th March 2018 (David)

It is only four days till my two-year anniversary of my second accident. It has been two years that have changed me in many ways. There are the obvious physical changes: pain, restriction in movement, and twelve months of having to rebuild what was lost in recovery. Yet, I think the biggest change was my will to not let this defeat me. I have found a mental strength that I did not previously have. I no longer fear pain. On the bike I can escape the memories and fight my way back to what I can now call 'normal.' Well, tomorrow is the next step with my first road race since the accident.

Journal Entry — Day 722: Wednesday 21st March 2018

Today marks two years since that awful day in 2016 that changed our lives so drastically. As I sit here and reflect on the past two years, I realise that most of 2016 is a blur of hospitals; doctor appointments; juggling work, business, and sporting commitments; spending hours clocking up thousands of kilometers up and down the highway between Shepparton and Melbourne; all whilst trying to keep it together for the kids.

The things that do stand out, however (and that I will never forget), are the boys who sat with David on that cold morning, keeping him calm until the emergency services got him out from under that vehicle and to hospital; the amazing paramedics, doctors and nurses who painstakingly put him back together; the phenomenal support and love from our family and friends (both existing and new); our local community in Toolamba and Shepparton; the cycling community; and the support and prayers of everyone who has followed our journey via our Facebook page, many of whom we have never met and probably never will.

I know without a shadow of a doubt we would not be where we are today without each and every one of you. So as we mark this two-year anniversary, I am filled with gratitude that David had the mental tenacity and stubbornness to fight to live, to learn to walk again, and to not let the daily challenges and constant pain and limitations stop him from being the best person he can be.

I am grateful for each person that has touched our lives in some way, big or small. I am thankful for the amazing opportunities that prompted our move from Victoria to South Australia in late September last year to create a fresh start for our family.

So as we embrace our new home and opportunities with open hearts and positive expectation, we will strive to be the best us we can be, to appreciate the small things day to day, to do our little bit to help those around us, and to never, ever give up on our dreams.

For no matter what life throws at us, we are survivors!

So, as you go through your day today, please remember to be grateful for the little things in life for they are by far the most important. From our family to yours…thank you!

Kylie Paton

Journal Entry — Day 784: Tuesday 22nd May 2018 (David)

Two years since those first steps were taken. Possibly the hardest thing I have ever had to do!

Yet I am reminded every day and do my best to remind others as well: "Surround yourself with the right people and never listen to anyone who says you cannot do something."

I hope you are lucky to have that special person beside you in life!

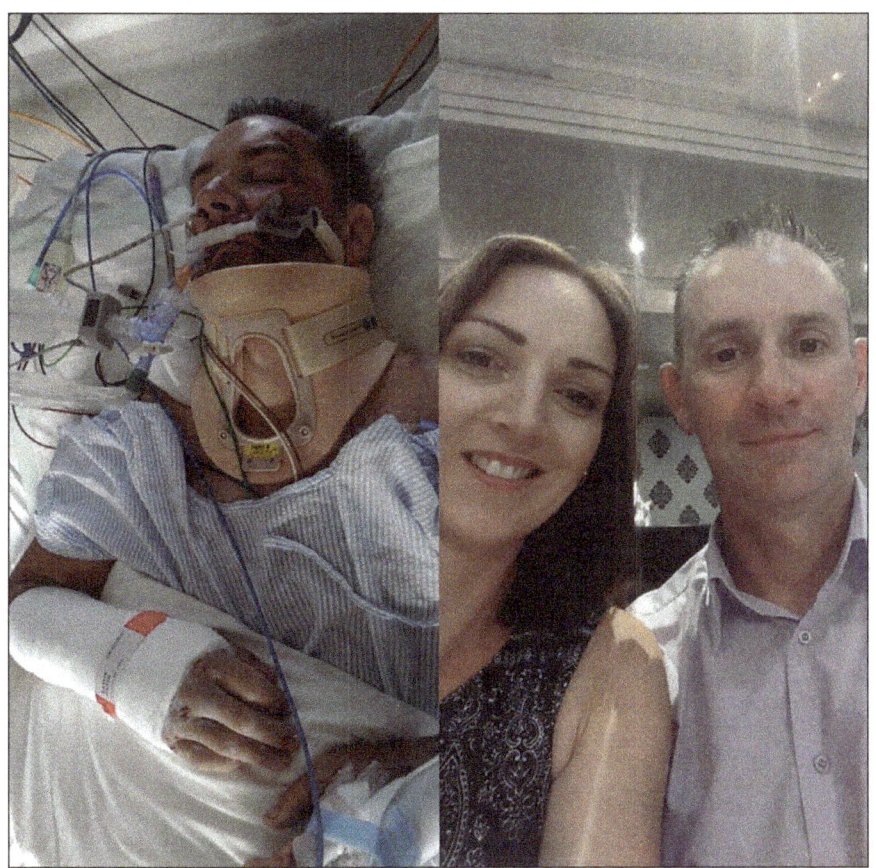

Reflecting on the journey from lying broken in a hospital bed to now.

Journal Entry — Day 808: Friday 15th June 2018 (David)

Just when you start to question where you are in life, the reason stares you in the face and says, "Buckle up for the ride!"

Journal Entry — Day 822: Friday 29th June 2018 (David)

Today I had the opportunity to share my journey with 60 Grade 4s. Mine is not a story about safety or blood and guts. It is a story about inspiration, resilience, hard work, and mindset.

About ten weeks after the accident I asked myself, "Why me?" Well, today I got my answer. It's not easy to keep the attention of 60 ten-year-olds, but I did! I told them that I was exactly where I am supposed to be, and they are my inspiration!

If you have the chance to be a positive influence on someone today, do it—that is more important than anything else you could achieve. Many great things have happened in my life, but perhaps lying under that car, nearly dying, was maybe the most important.

Joshua's teacher had asked David if he would be willing to assist in Joshua's classroom with teaching the kids who were struggling with their times tables. This led to David becoming a mentor in the Learning Assistance Program (LAP) the school runs. He mentored a number of the kids one-on-one for the year and still to this day works with two of the children. This was and is a great opportunity for both David and the kids he's mentored!

Journal Entry — Day 825: Monday 2nd July 2018 (David)

Be someone's inspiration today. You do not have to rise from the dead to be an inspiration; you simply have to make a difference.

I find myself again being sucked into the helmet argument. Whether it is compulsory or not, just wear one! I am yet to have anyone give me a legitimate reason for not wearing one, other than insisting it's their right to choose not to.

A reminder of what David's helmet looked like after the accident.
If he hadn't worn one, he would be dead.

Journal Entry — Day 990: Thursday 13th December 2018 (David)

Thanks to Grade 4H. These kids think it is about me helping them; how surprised they would be to know how big an impact they have on me!

There are days where knowing they are waiting for me is the only reason to get out of bed!

Football of David's favorite team signed by all the kids in Grade 4H.

CREATING A NEW 'NORMAL' | 155

Journal Entry — Day 1001: Monday 24th December 2018 (David)

I believe that I was chosen to go through what I did (yes, I really do!) so that I could find my way. Below is a note from a ten-year-old who I can now call a friend, but I had no idea the impact I had on them. This is my reason; this is why I was chosen.

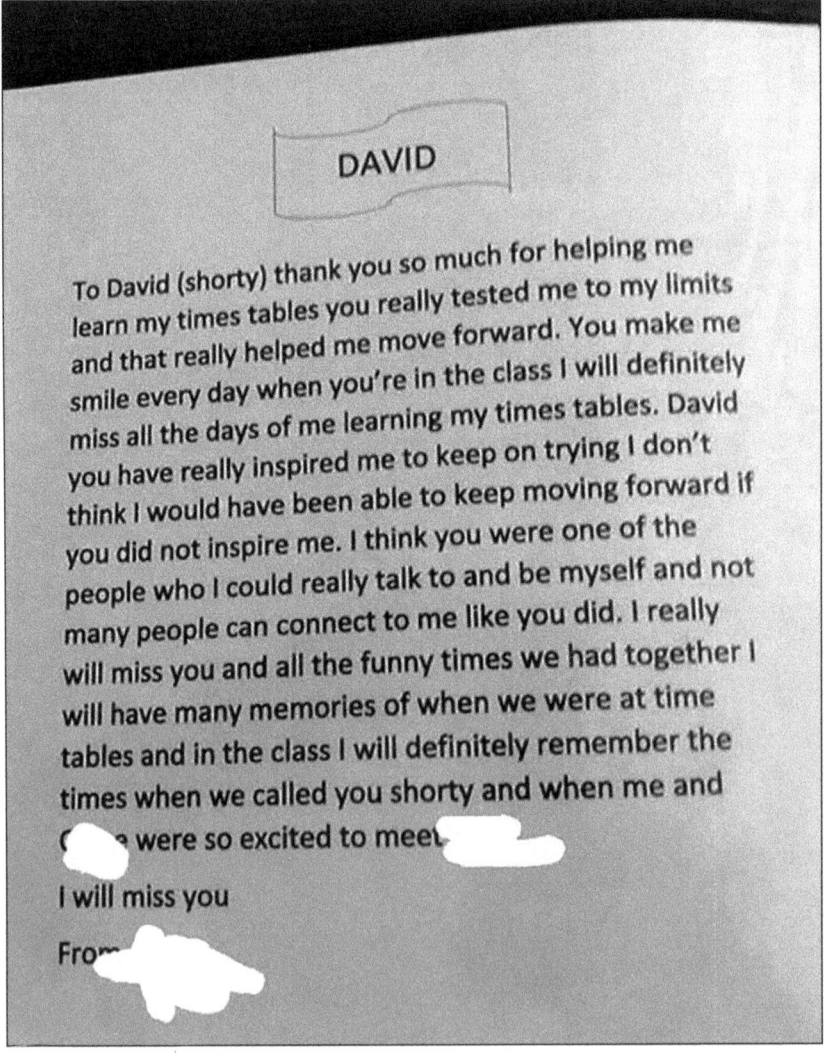

A note from a ten-year-old whose life David impacted.

Journal Entry — Day 1049: Sunday 10th February (David)

Journal Entry — Day 1064: Monday 25th February 2019 (David)

Dear God: Burn every bridge in my life that leads my life back to destruction.

Journal Entry — Day 1088: Thursday 21st March 2019

It is hard to believe it has been three years since David's second cycling accident. I have been writing our story over the last twelve months and it has brought tears, laughter, and the always present question, "Why us?" The funny thing is that every time that question pops into my head, I always get the same answer: "Why not us?"

Whether my story ever makes it into print and onto bookstore shelves, or remains on my laptop for my kids and grandkids to read one day, it has taught me a lot of things.

It has taught me that we are blessed, and that life is short—don't take it for granted. It has taught me that there are still good people in this world, and that in every tough situation there is always a silver lining. It may not be readily apparent at the time and it may be years before you are in a healthy enough place to recognize it, but it will be there somewhere.

In our case, the trauma and the hardships caused by this event have been huge, and their impact will affect us for the rest of our lives. There are mental and emotional scars that we are all still working through and trying to heal; and for David, the physical limitations and pain are a daily reminder of all he has lost.

That being said, what he has gained in the process is nothing short of remarkable. He has found his purpose in life; and out of a tragedy, he is now making a difference in the lives of many kids through a mentorship program at our children's school. To hear David talk about 'his kids,' as he refers to them, fills my heart with joy and makes those days just a little easier to bear.

So, on this three-year anniversary, I implore you all to never lose sight of what is possible. It is very easy to wallow in what has been lost and no one would blame you for that, but it makes for a very unfulfilled and potentially lonely existence. Search for the nuggets, reach out, and ask for help. Do not let the hurts define your future; stand up and fight for a better now with what you have to work with.

Will it be easy? Probably not!

Will it be worth it? Yes!

Sending my love and prayers to you all.

Journal Entry — Day 1187: Wednesday 28th August 2019 (David)

Do not tell me you cannot!!!

Epilogue

22nd December 2019

I am sitting here on the banks of the Murray River in South Punyelroo, South Australia, reflecting on the journey that has bought us to this point in our lives. As the 4th anniversary of David's accident looms, I am grateful for the people (old and new) in our life. For the lessons—hard, and often painful—that we have learned, and most of all for the love and grace that helped us to survive what life has thrown at us.

I am extremely grateful to be married to a man who does not understand the meaning of 'giving up,' and I'm grateful for the two resilient, strong, and, at times, frustrating kids we are raising.

The banks of the Murray River.

So, as I sit here pondering our journey, I am reminded of these quotes:

> Family isn't always blood. It's the people in your life who want you in theirs. The ones who accept you for who you are. The ones who would do anything to see you smile, and who love you no matter what.
>
> - Unknown

But even with the stress and hardship that has been our life, I am so grateful for every blessing that has come our way. I hope that, as you have read these pages, you have found some hope to keep going, a strength you did not know you had, and a determination to not let life's obstacles define you—no matter what you are facing. Life does not always go the way we've planned or hoped, but it is up to us to decide how to react to it.

I do not know what the future holds for David, Kaitlyn, Joshua, and myself, but what I do know is that we will continue to love, laugh, fight, and support each other—no matter what the journey ahead looks like.

I wish you every happiness, and may God bless each and every one of you.

Love, Kylie xx

August 5th 2020 – A final word from David

I wake up every morning to scars that remind me of the battle, so why not make it permanent with some ink?

Thank you for sharing our journey with us; keep smiling, keep fighting, and never, ever give up!

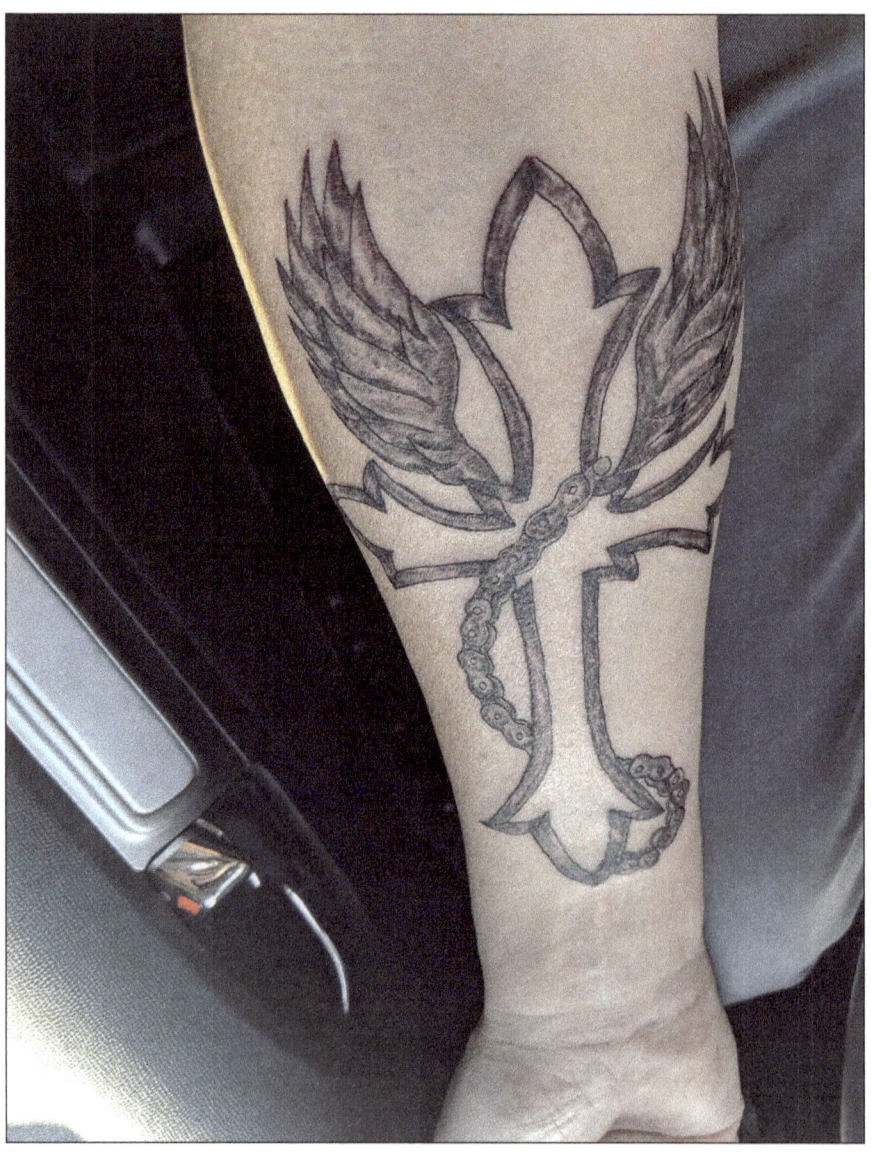

Acknowledgments

Firstly, I want to thank God, for without His will for David to still be here on earth, I have no doubt that he would be in heaven right now.

To the staff at The Alfred Hospital and Epworth Rehabilitation Hospital Camberwell, Pete and Prue, Tan, Mum and Dad Jemmeson, Mum and Dad Paton, Dot and Ian, Matt & Joles, Peter and Lynne, the Prayer Warriors, the Shepparton Cycling Community, the Toolamba Community, all our friends and family, and the thousands of people who have followed our journey and prayed for our family—thank you. This book is for you. It is only with your support, love, prayers, and encouragement that we have survived the challenges that life has thrown at us.

To Kaitlyn and Joshua, thank you for your resilience, your tenacity, and your belief that Daddy would get better against all the odds. You are my life, and I am so thankful for the strength that you have shown through the ups and downs of our journey. I love you.

And last but certainly not least to my husband, thank you for being too stubborn to die and for refusing to accept the lot that was handed to you. You barreled into my life and it has been a roller coaster ride ever since. You have taught me to not take myself so seriously, to pick my fights and to embrace the unknown. We have loved, laughed, fought, and cried, but throughout it all we have never given up on us, on our family, or on God and His will for our lives. Your resilience and refusal to let life's challenges beat you down is inspirational. I love you.

The End

January 2021

Mental Health Support Services

Adult

Lifeline: 13 11 14
lifeline.org.au

Suicide Call Back Service: 1300 659 469
suicidecallbackservice.org.au

Beyond Blue: 1300 224 636
beyondblue.org.au

MensLine Australia: 1300 789 978
mensline.org.au

Black Dog Institute:
Blackdoginstitute.org.au

Youth

Kids Helpline: 1800 551 800
kidshelpline.com.au

Headspace: 1800 650 890
headspace.org.au

Other Resources

Children of Parents with Mental Illness:
copmi.net.au

Lifeline: 13 11 14
lifeline.org.au

Relationships Australia: 1300 364 277
relationships.org.au

www.ingramcontent.com/pod-product-compliance
Lightning Source LLC
Chambersburg PA
CBHW062027290426
44108CB00025B/2803